65 Birdhouses and Bird Feeders
...For All Bird Lovers To Build

Ronald D. Tarjany

Tarjany Publications
PO Box 8846 Calabasas CA 91302

Copyright © 2001 by Tarjany Publications

This book may not be reproduced, either in part or in its entirety, in any form, by any means, without permission from the publisher, with the exception of brief exerpts for the purpose of radio, television, or published reviews. Although all possible measures have been taken to ensure the accuracy of the material presented, neither the author nor Tarjany Publications is liable in case of misinterpretation of directions, misapplication or typographical error. All rights, including the right of translation, are reserved.

Printed in United States of America

10 9 8 7 6 5 4 3 2 1
First Edition

ISBN 0-9674668-4-9

This Book was Produced by
TARJANY PUBLICATIONS
PO Box 8846, Calabasas, CA 91302

Editor: Cathy Starbird
Copy Editor: Kitty Lane
Design: Les Ventura
Illustrations: David R. Shea
Cover ilustrations: Julian Argon

Library of Congress Cataloging-in-Publication Data

Tarjany, Ronald D.
   65 Birdhouses and Bird Feeders: For All Bird Lovers To Build

  Includes index.
  ISBN 0-9674668-4-9
  1. Birdhouses---Design.
  2. Bird Feeders---Design.
  I. Title. II. Title: 65 Birdhouses and Bird Feeders: For All Bird Lovers To Build
  Library of Congress Control Number: 2001130574

Contents

Author's Notes 4
Plans

1 Small Hanging Bird Feeder 5
2 Typical Birdhouse 6
3 Wall Mounted Bluebird Birdhouse 7
4 Bluebird Birdhouse 8
5 Diamond Birdhouse for Wrens 9
6 Wall Mounted Bird Feeder 10
7 Three-Tier Birdhouse for Wrens . . . 11
8 Wall Mounted Nesting Shelf for Robins 12
9 Log Cabin Birdhouse 13
10 Hanging Bird Feeder 14
11 Post Bird Feeder 15
12 Window Bird Feeder 16
13 PVC Pipe Birdhouse 16
14 Flower-Pot Birdhouse 16
15 Post Mounted Hopper Bird Feeder . . . 17
16 Barn Birdhouse for Wrens 18
17 Three Station Bird Feeder 19
18 Eight-Apartment Martin Birdhouse . . 20
19 Hanging Bird Feeder 22
20 A-Frame Birdhouse 23
21 School House Birdhouse 24
22 Dove Cove 25
23 Church Birdhouse 26
24 Mailbox Birdhouse 27
25 16-Apartment Martin Birdhouse 28
26 Farm House Birdhouse 29
27 Post Bird Feeder 30
28 Hopper Bird Feeder 31
29 Log Shed Birdhouse 32
30 Birdhouse for Tree Swallows 33
31 Tree Swallow Birdhouse 34
32 Robin Nesting Shelf 35
33 Log House Birdhouse 36
34 Church Birdhouse 37
35 8-Sided Martin Birdhouse 38
36 Triangle Dove Cove 40
37 Adobe Birdhouse 41
38 Two Dwelling Birdhouse 42
39 Nesting Shelf 43
40 Bird Feeding Table 43
41 18-Apartment Martin Birdhouse 44
42 Four Post Bird Feeder 46
43 Three-Tier Bird Feeder 47
44 Slab Log Cabin Birdhouse 48
45 Modern High-Rise Building Birdhouse . 49
46 Old Western Building Birdhouse 50
47 Railroad Crummy Birdhouse 51
48 Old House Birdhouse 52
49 Wall Clock Birdhouse 53
50 Shingle Roof Birdhouse 54
51 PVC Pipe Bird Feeder 55
52 Hanging Birdhouse from Logs 55
53 Triangle Birdhouse 56
54 Hanging Wire Cage Suet Feeder 57
55 Rustic Bird Feeder 57
56 Fruit Bird Feeder 57
57 Bird Feeder of Logs 58
58 Log Birdhouse for Woodpeckers 59
59 Round Hanging Platform Feeder 59
60 Wren House Birdhouse 60
61 Glass Jar Bird Feeder 61
62 Suet Wall Feeder 61
63 Suet Log Bird Feeder 62
64 Hanging Water Bath 62
65 Wall Bird Feeder 62
Birdhouse Size Requirements. 63
Index 64

Author's Notes

Bird watching is an enjoyable pastime – and the best way to bring those birds into your backyard garden is to add a bird feeder to attract the birds. One bird feeder will draw several birds through the day and many species. After the birds are in your backyard garden they will need a house to nest. This will lead to building more bird feeders and birdhouses as the population explodes and your bird watching becomes more enjoyable.

Over the years I have made hundreds of sketches of birdhouses and bird feeders. I used these sketches to build some of the houses and put others aside for another time. I would go through these sketches and get new ideas and sketch up another design. Finally I got all these sketches together and picked a good sampling of the many design. I refined these sketches and turned them into finished drawings and thus was born this book *65 Birdhouses and Bird Feeders*. The designs cover the small, medium and very large structures

The birdhouse and bird feeder designs in this book can be built from any type of wood. Redwood and western red cedar are good choices and will last many years in the cruelest of climates. Construction grade plywood is also a good choice and scraps can often be found around construction sites. Ask the building foreman for permission before hauling away any of the scrap. Plywood will need a preservative or paint to make it last in the elements.

SMALL HANGING BIRD FEEDER

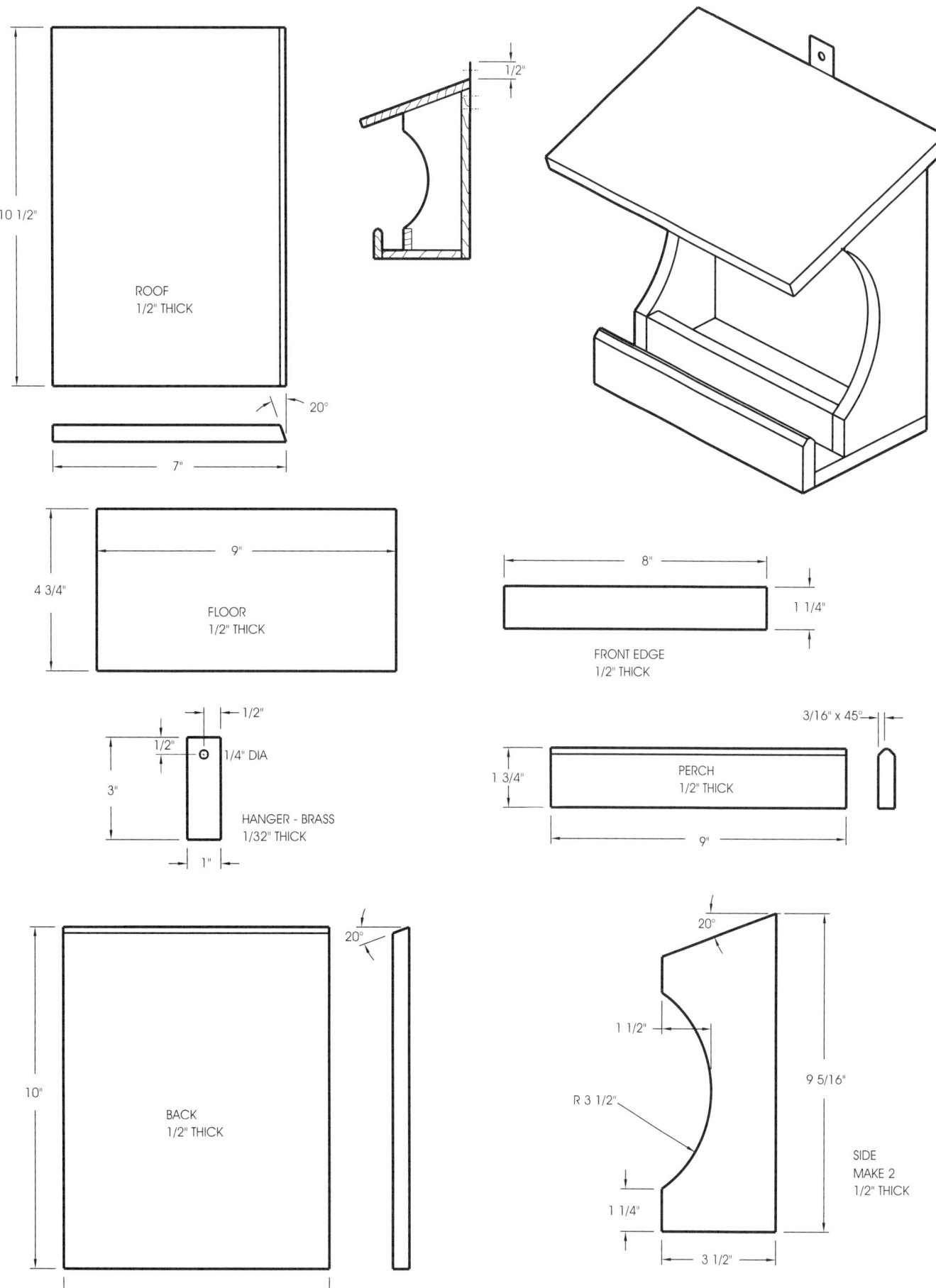

TYPICAL BIRDHOUSE

3/4" ROOF OVERHANG FRONT AND BACK

REMOVABLE ROOF

2" DIA PIPE AND PIPE FLOOR FLANGE ATTACHED TO BOTTOM OF BIRDHOUSE

FRONT 3/4" THICK
- 1 1/2" DIA
- 3 1/4"
- 2"
- 1/4" DIA
- 6"
- 5 1/2"
- 9 1/4"
- 6 1/2"

FLOOR 3/4" THICK
- 6"
- 5"

PERCH
- 2 1/2"
- 1/4" DIA

BACK 3/4" THICK
- 1/2"
- 3 1/4"
- 1 7/8"
- 1/4" DIA VENT HOLES
- 6"
- 9 1/4"
- 6 1/2"

ROOF 3/4" THICK
- 9"
- 6"

ROOF 3/4" THICK
- 9"
- 6 3/4"

SIDE MAKE 2 3/4" THICK
- 45°
- 6 3/4"
- 6"

WALL MOUNTED BLUEBIRD BIRDHOUSE

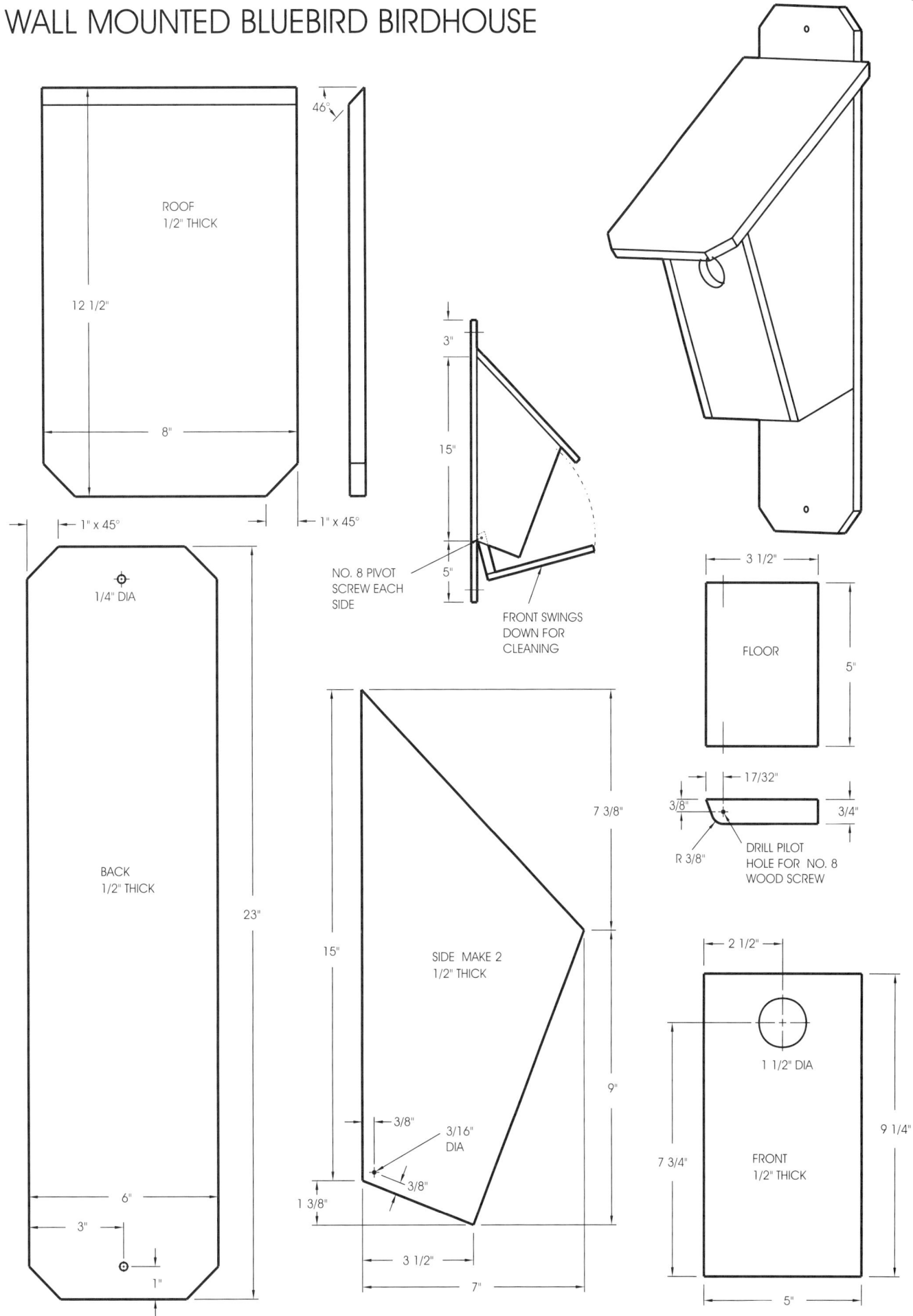

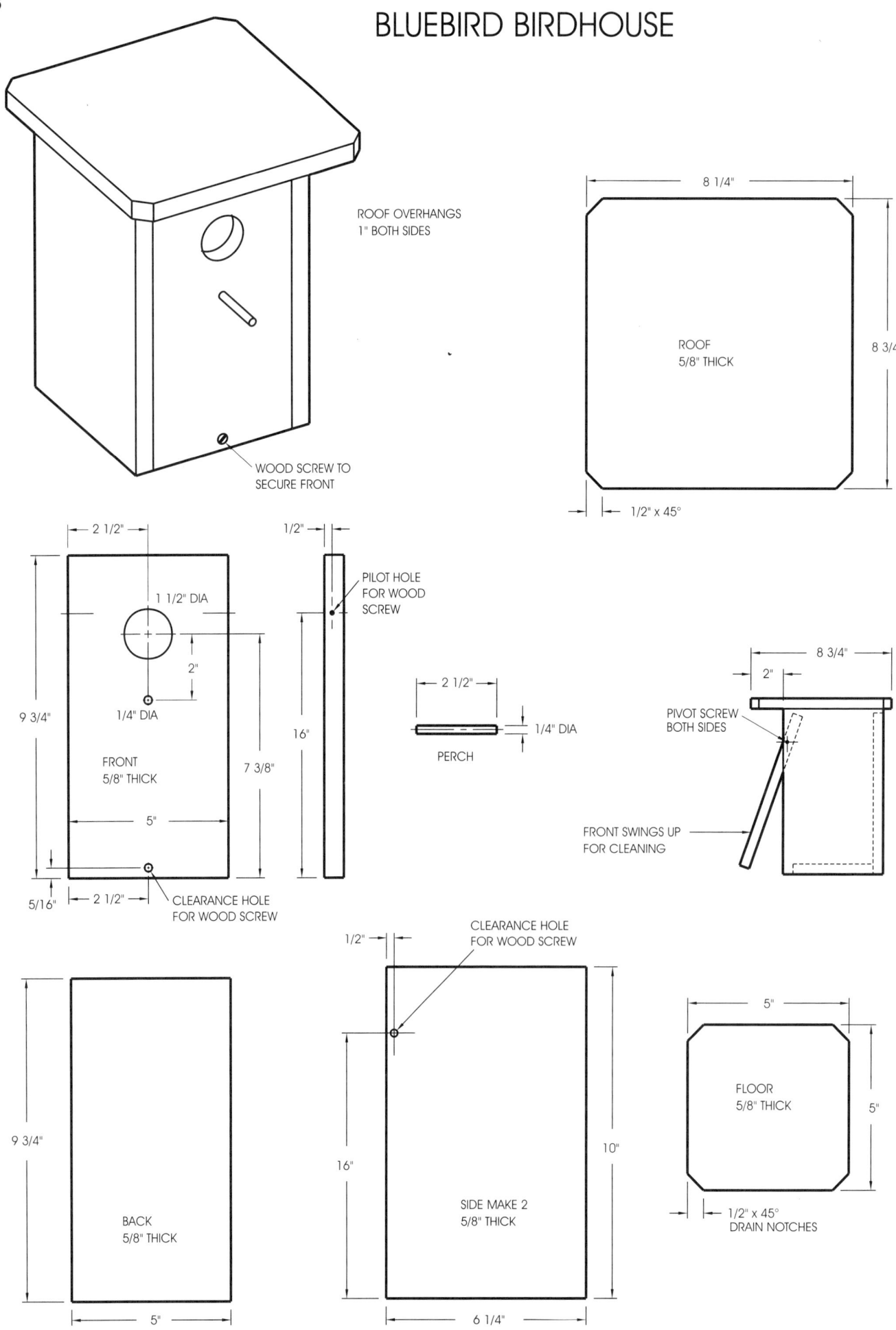

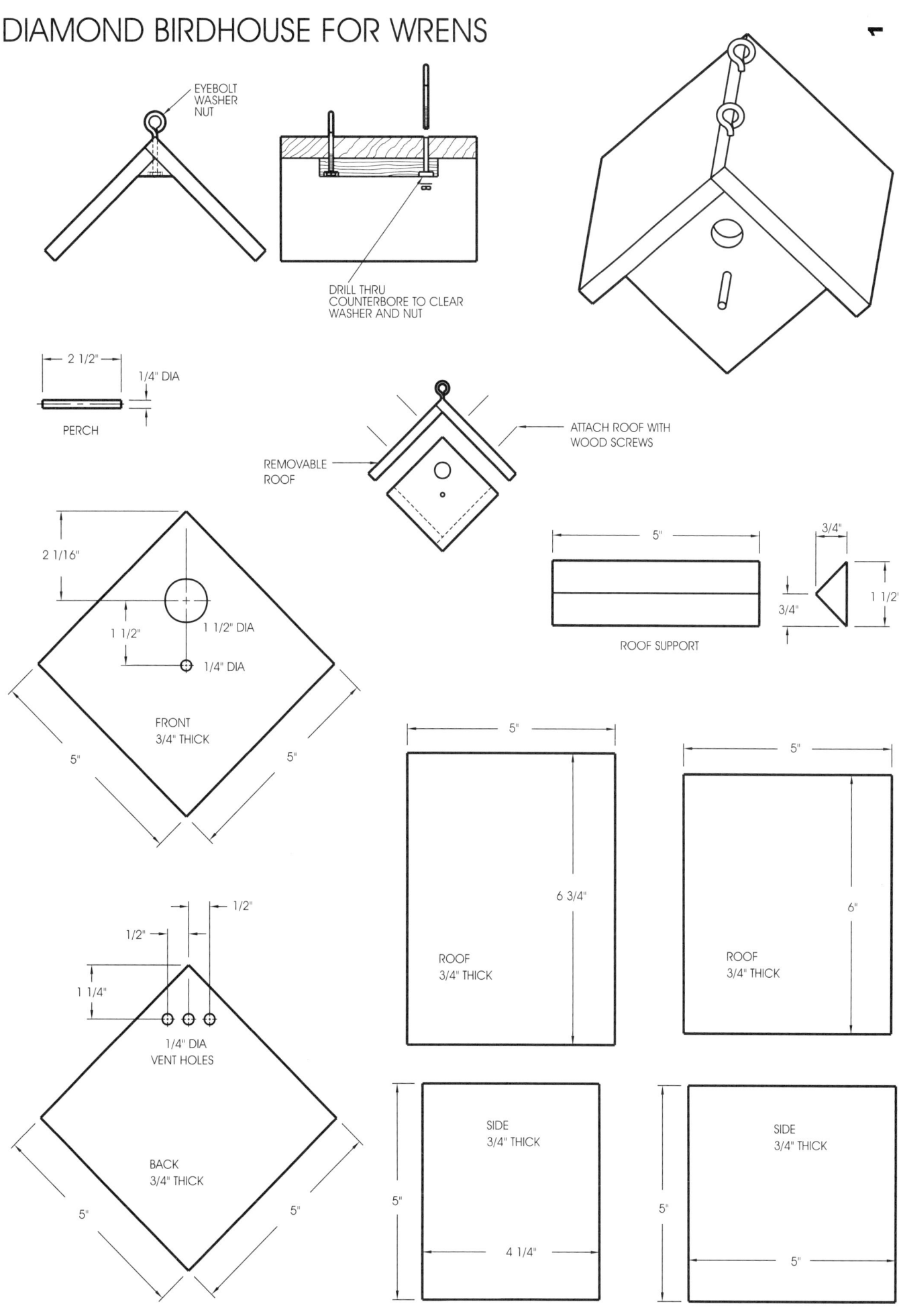

WALL MOUNTED BIRD FEEDER

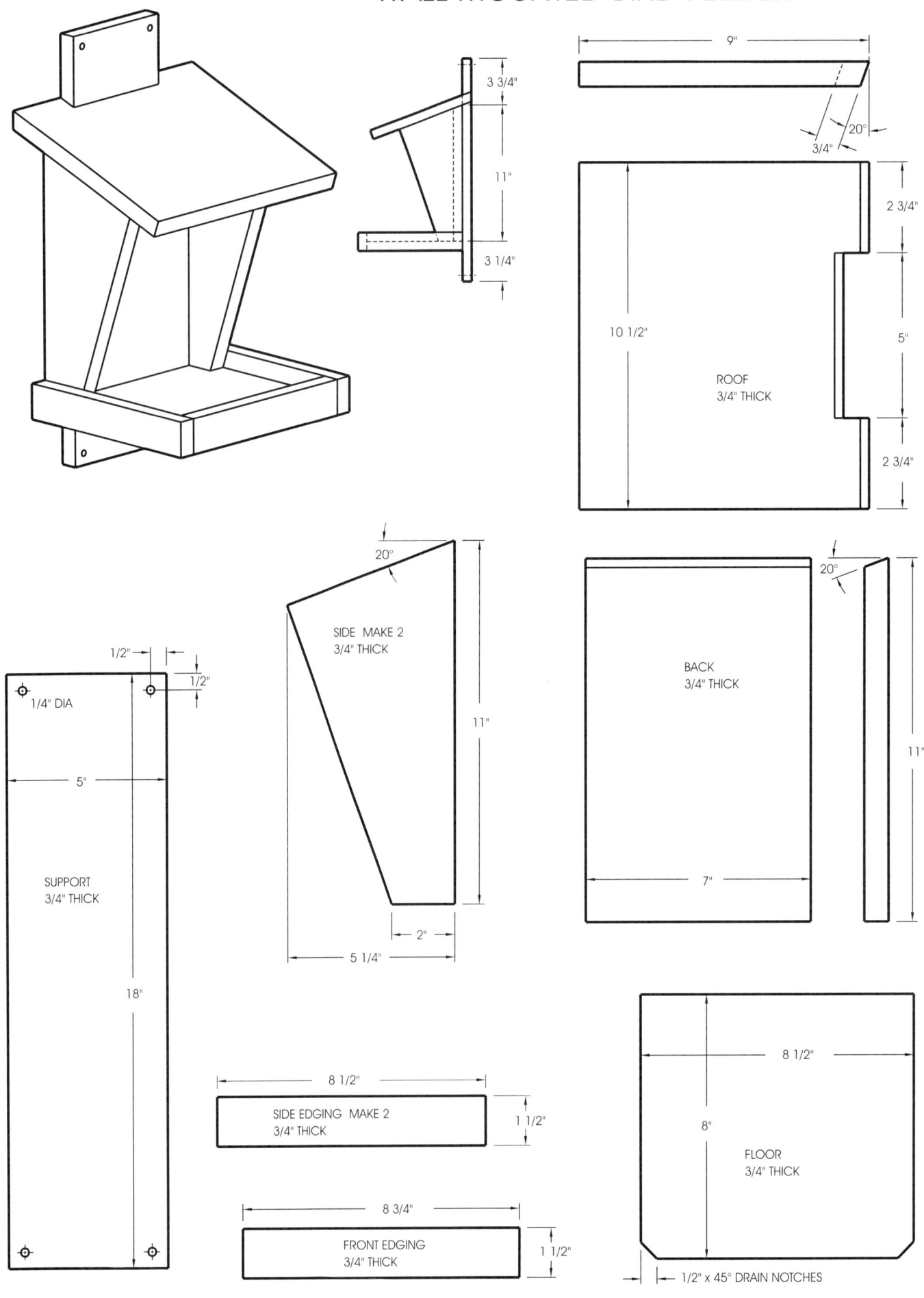

THREE-TIER BIRDHOUSE FOR WRENS

PERCH MAKE 3 — 2 1/2", 1", 1/4" x 45°

TOP CAP 3/4" THICK — 1/4" x 45°, 3/4", 3 1/2" DIA

LEFT SIDE 3/8" THICK — 1/2", 1", 1", 1", 1", 7 1/4", 22 1/2", 4", 1/4" DIA VENT HOLES, 1 1/4" DIA, 2", 3 3/4"

FRONT 3/8" THICK — 4 3/4", 1 1/4" DIA, 2 3/8", 11"

CAP MAKE 2, 3/4" THICK — 6", 6", 3/4" x 45°

2" SQUARE WOOD POST

RIGHT SIDE 3/8" THICK — 2", 4 1/4", 1 1/4" DIA, 4", VENT HOLES 1/4" DIA, 22 1/2", 7 1/4", 1/2", 1", 1", 1", 4"

REMOVABLE BACK 3/8" THICK — 4 3/4", 6 1/2", DRAIN HOLES 1/4" DIA, 1/8", 3/4", 5/8", 3 1/2", 6 1/2", 1/8", 3/4", 6 1/2", 1/8", 3/4"

FLOOR MAKE 4, 3/4" THICK — 4", 4"

POST CAP 3/4" THICK — 4 3/4", 4 3/4"

11

WALL MOUNTED NESTING SHELF FOR ROBINS

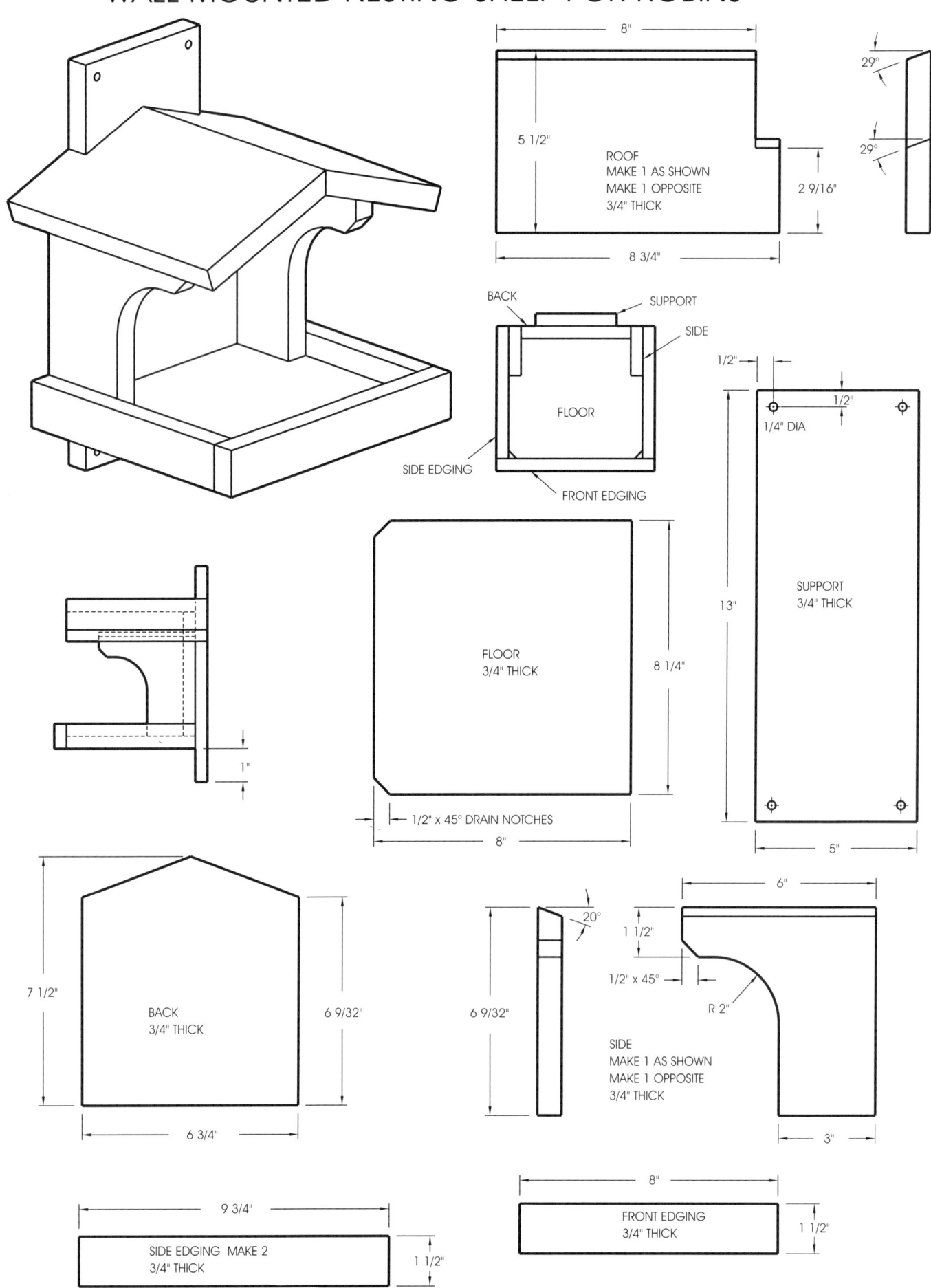

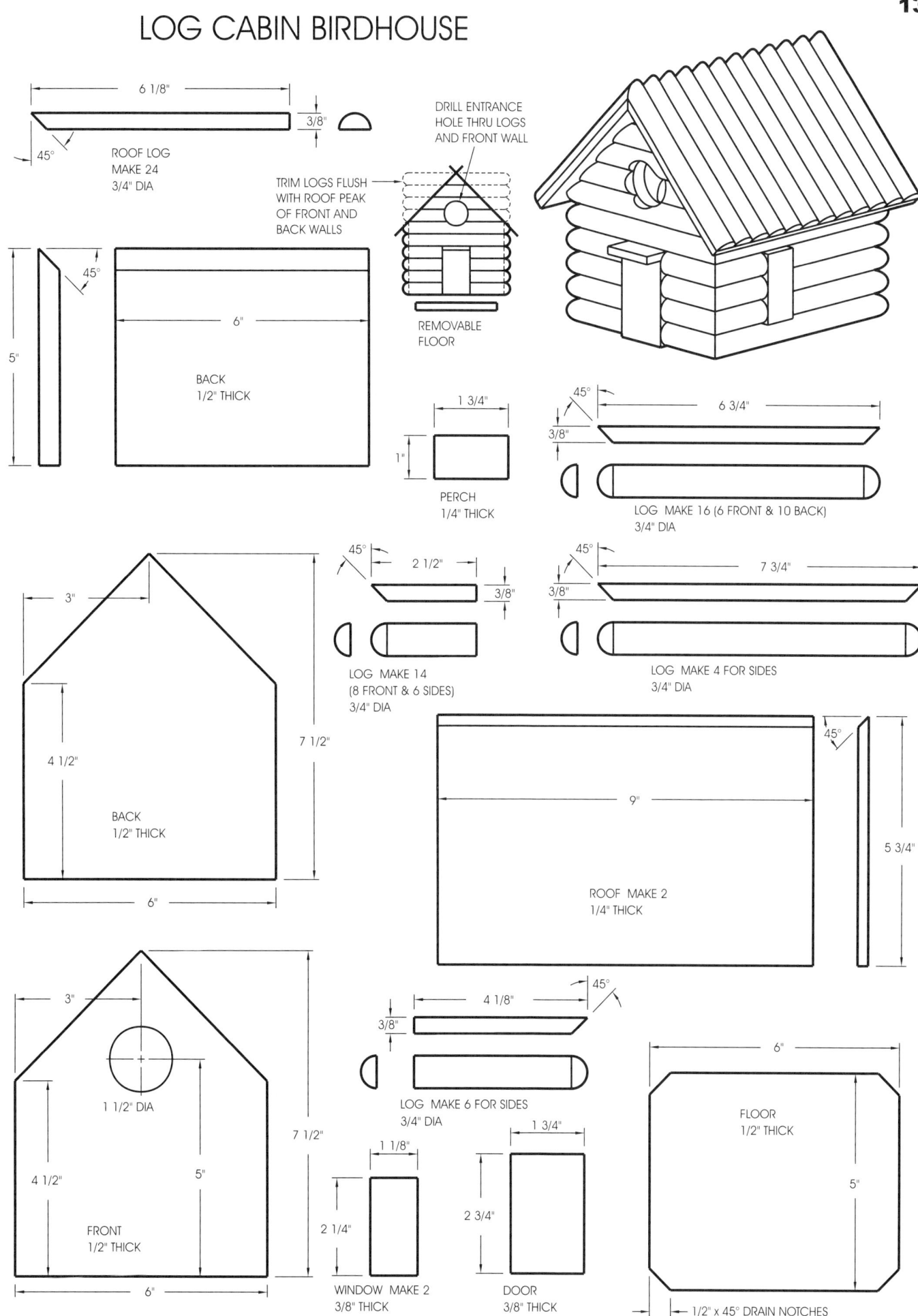

HANGING BIRD FEEDER

ROOF 1/2" THICK
- 9"
- 6 1/2"
- 4 1/2"
- 3"
- 3/16" DIA

HANGING HARDWARE
- EYEBOLT
- WASHER
- NUT

1"

BACK 1/2" THICK
- 7"
- 4 1/2"
- 30°

SLOPING BACK 1/4" THICK
- 7 1/2"
- 5 11/32"
- 30°
- 30°

FRONT GLASS 1/8" THICK
- 7 1/4"
- 4"

SPACER MAKE 2 1/4" THICK
- 1"
- 1/2"

5"

1/4"

SIDE MAKE 2 1/2" THICK
- 1/4" SAWCUT 1/4" DEEP
- 1/8" SAWCUT 1/8" DEEP
- 4 1/2"
- 1 5/8"
- 30°

FLOOR 1/2" THICK
- 10"
- 9"

POST BIRD FEEDER

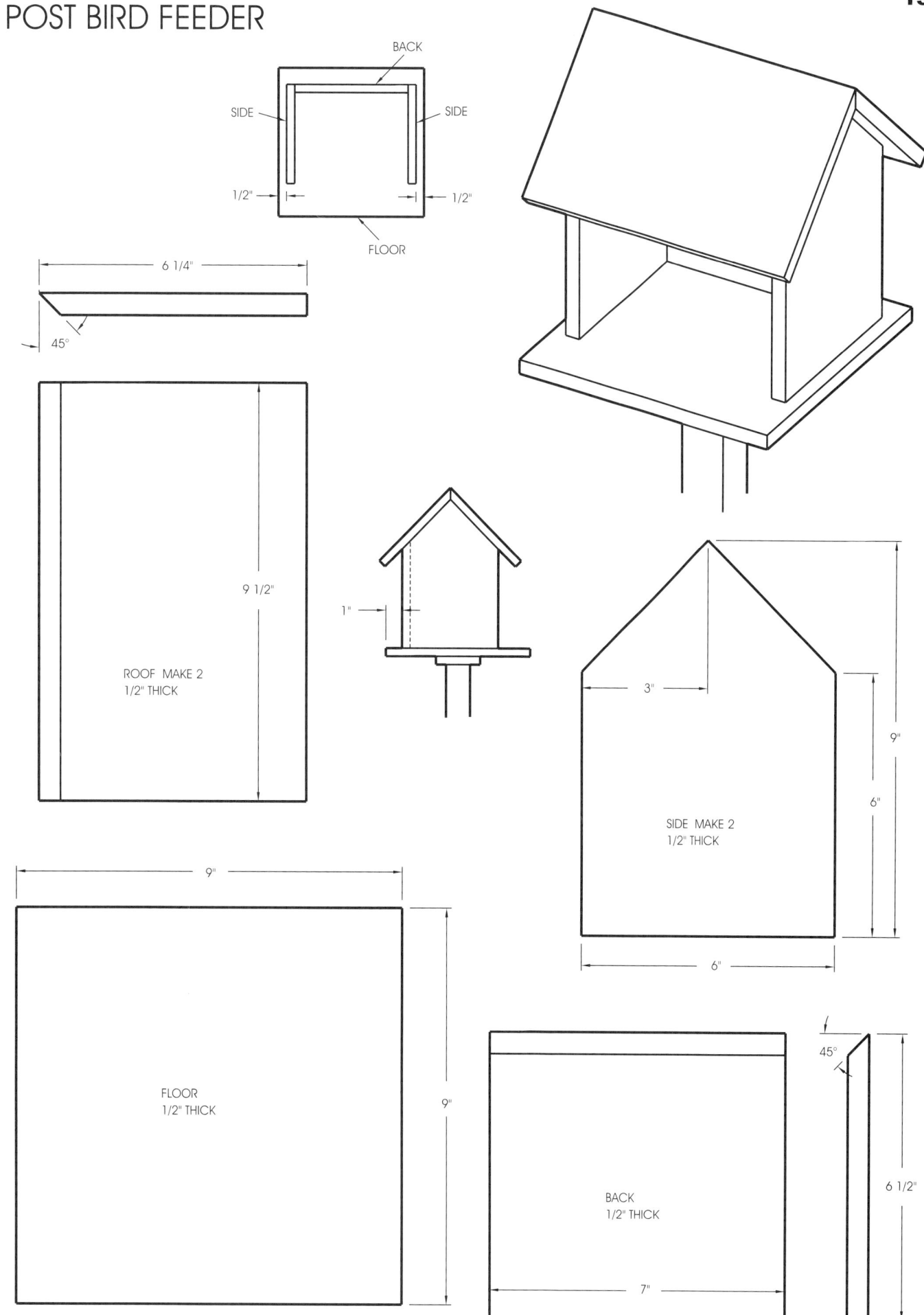

WINDOW BIRD FEEDER

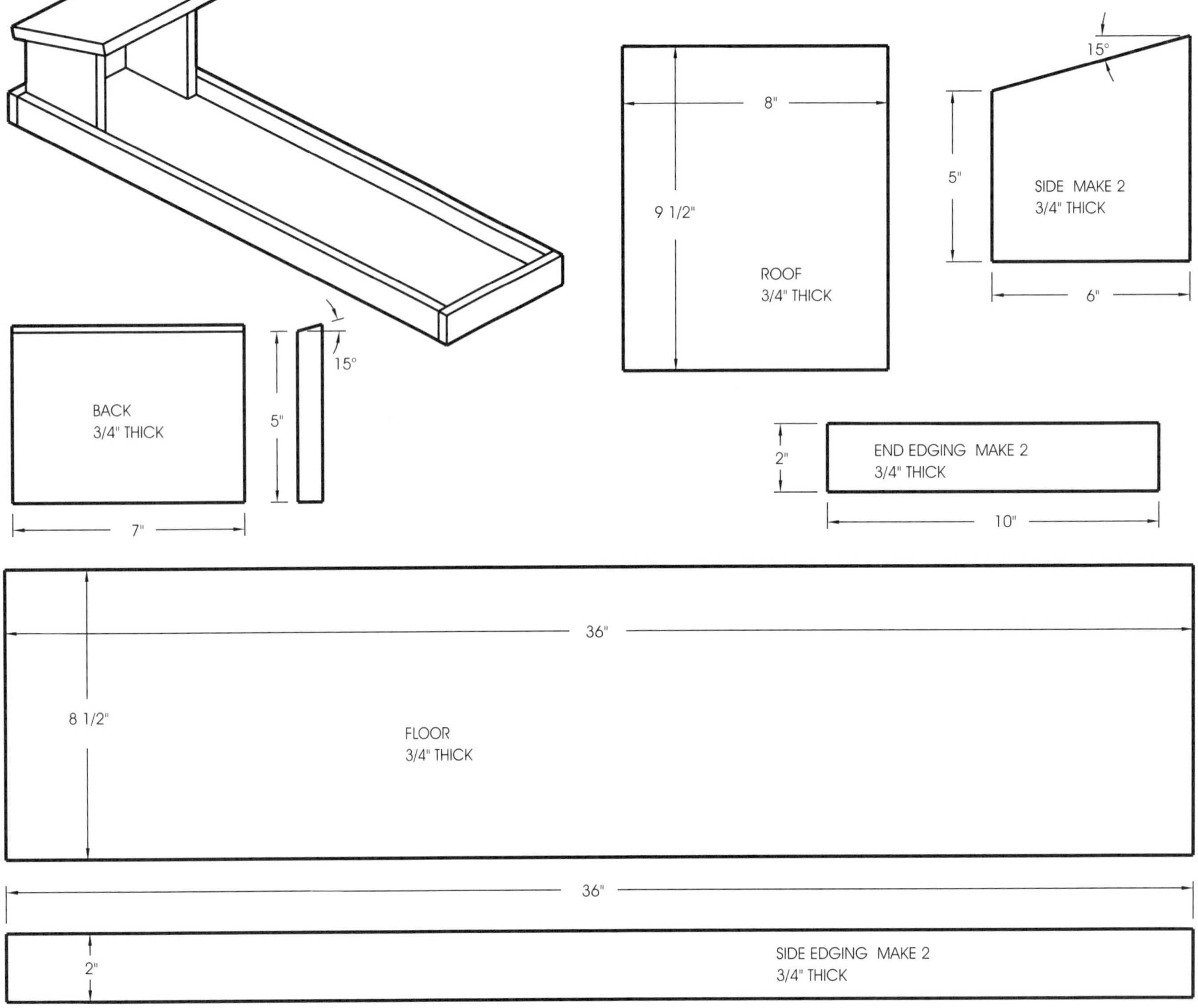

- BACK 3/4" THICK — 7" × 5", 15°
- ROOF 3/4" THICK — 8" × 9 1/2"
- SIDE MAKE 2, 3/4" THICK — 6" × 5", 15°
- END EDGING MAKE 2, 3/4" THICK — 10" × 2"
- FLOOR 3/4" THICK — 36" × 8 1/2"
- SIDE EDGING MAKE 2, 3/4" THICK — 36" × 2"

PVC PIPE BIRDHOUSE

- PVC PIPE TO SUIT
- 1 1/4" DIA ENTRANCE HOLE
- PERCH 3/8" DIA, 1 3/4" LONG
- BACK WALL 3/4" THICK
- FRONT WALL 3/4" THICK

FLOWER-POT BIRDHOUSE

- 1 1/4" DIA ENTRANCE HOLE
- PERCH 3/8" DIA, 1 3/4" LONG
- FRONT WALL 3/4" THICK
- FLOWER-POT TO SUIT

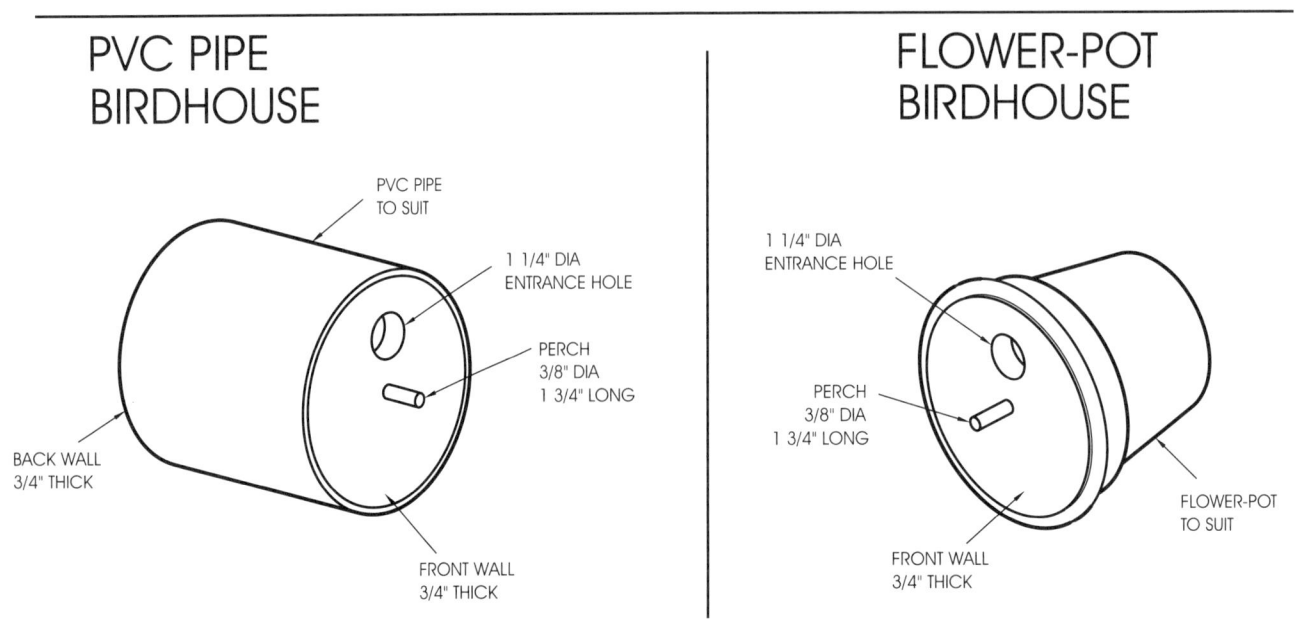

POST MOUNTED HOPPER BIRD FEEDER

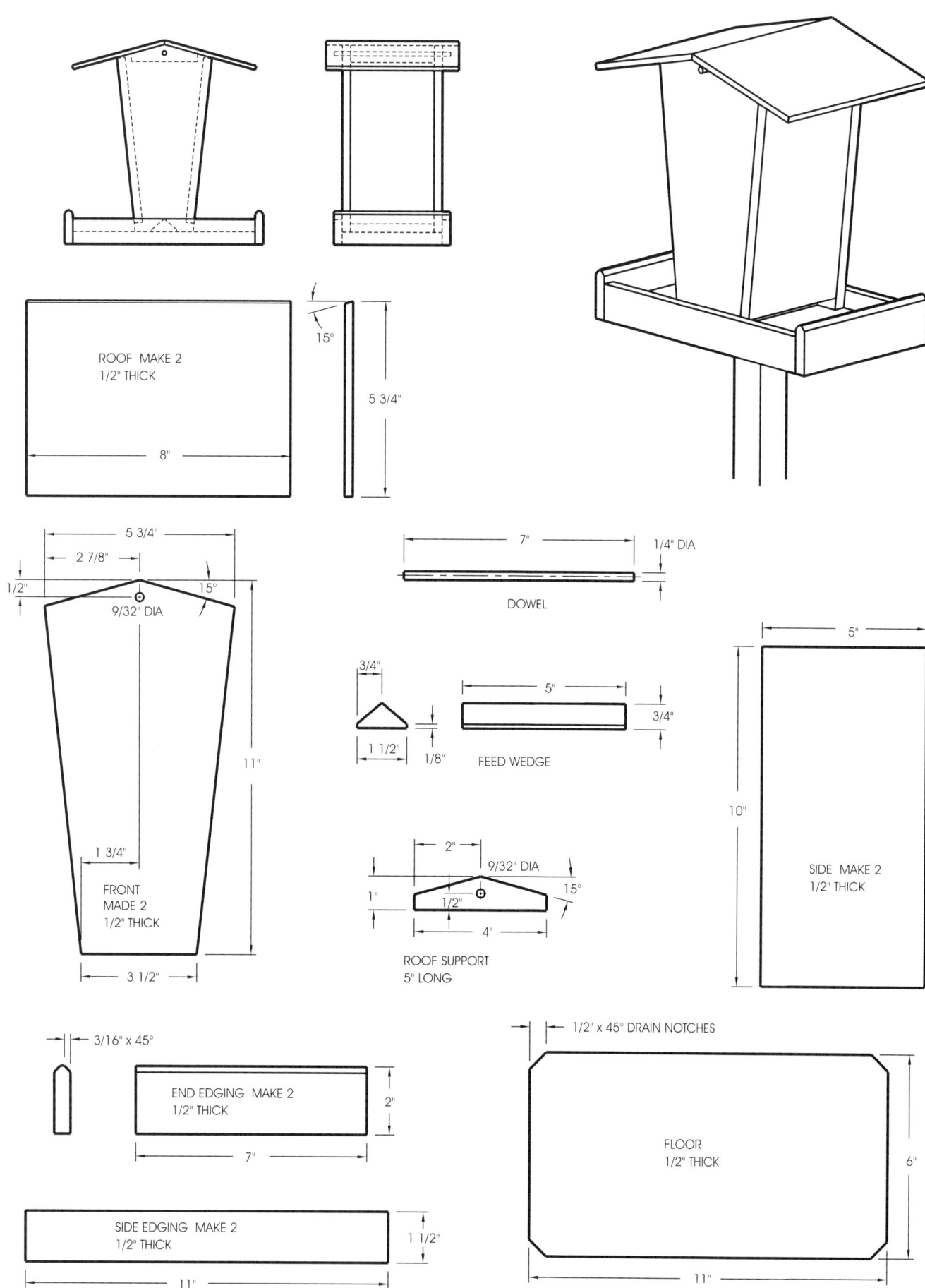

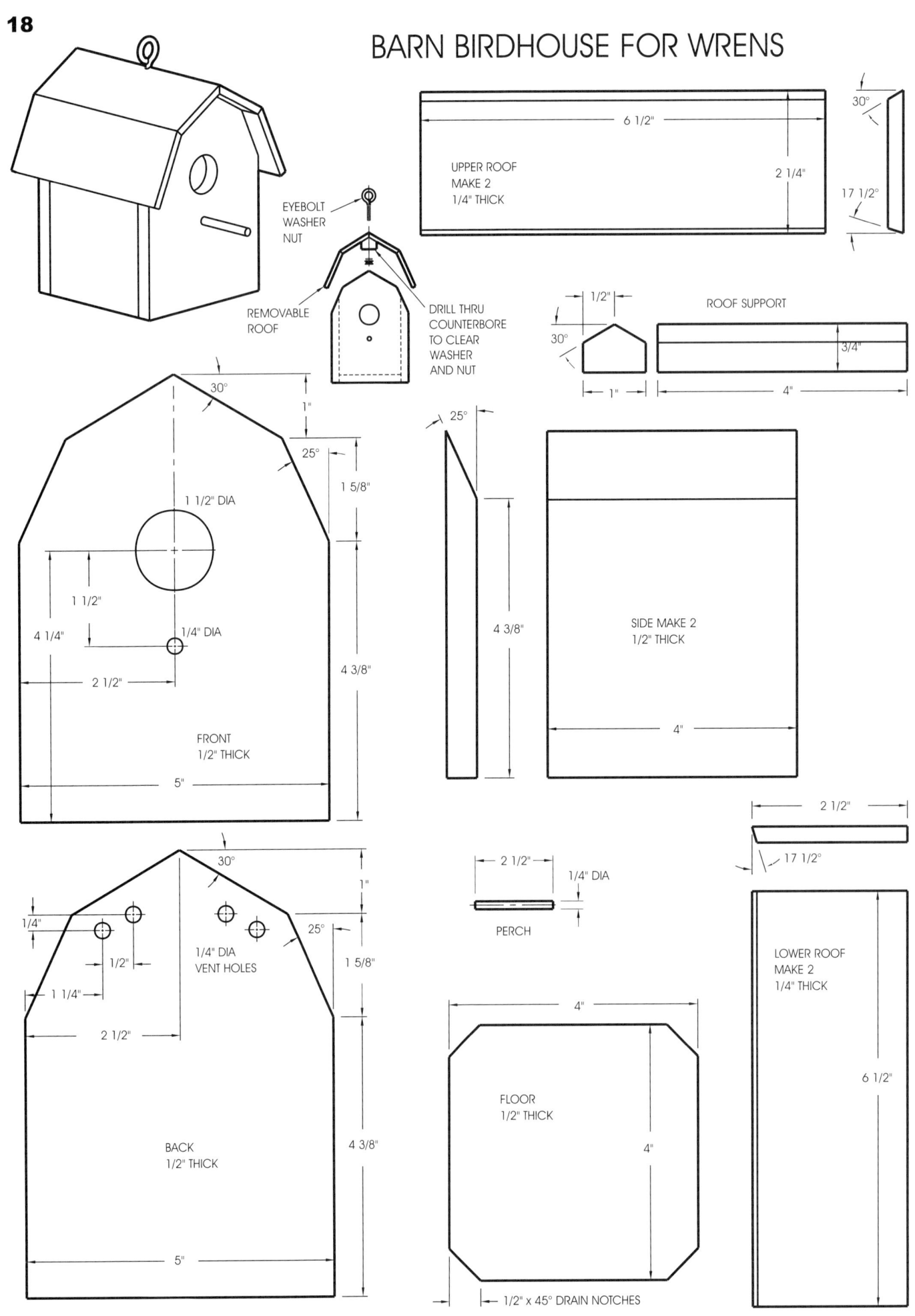

THREE STATION BIRD FEEDER

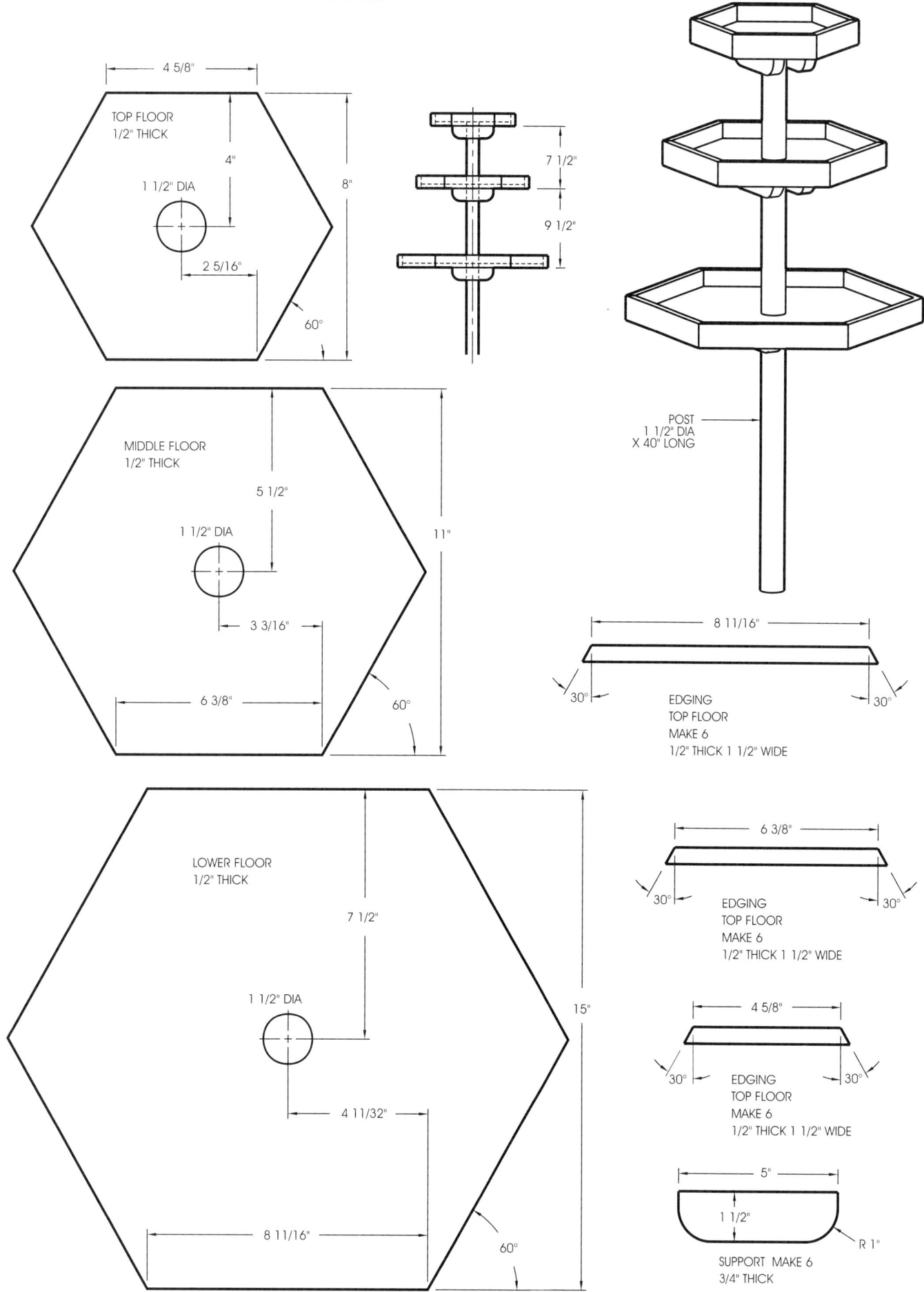

EIGHT-APARTMENT MARTIN BIRDHOUSE

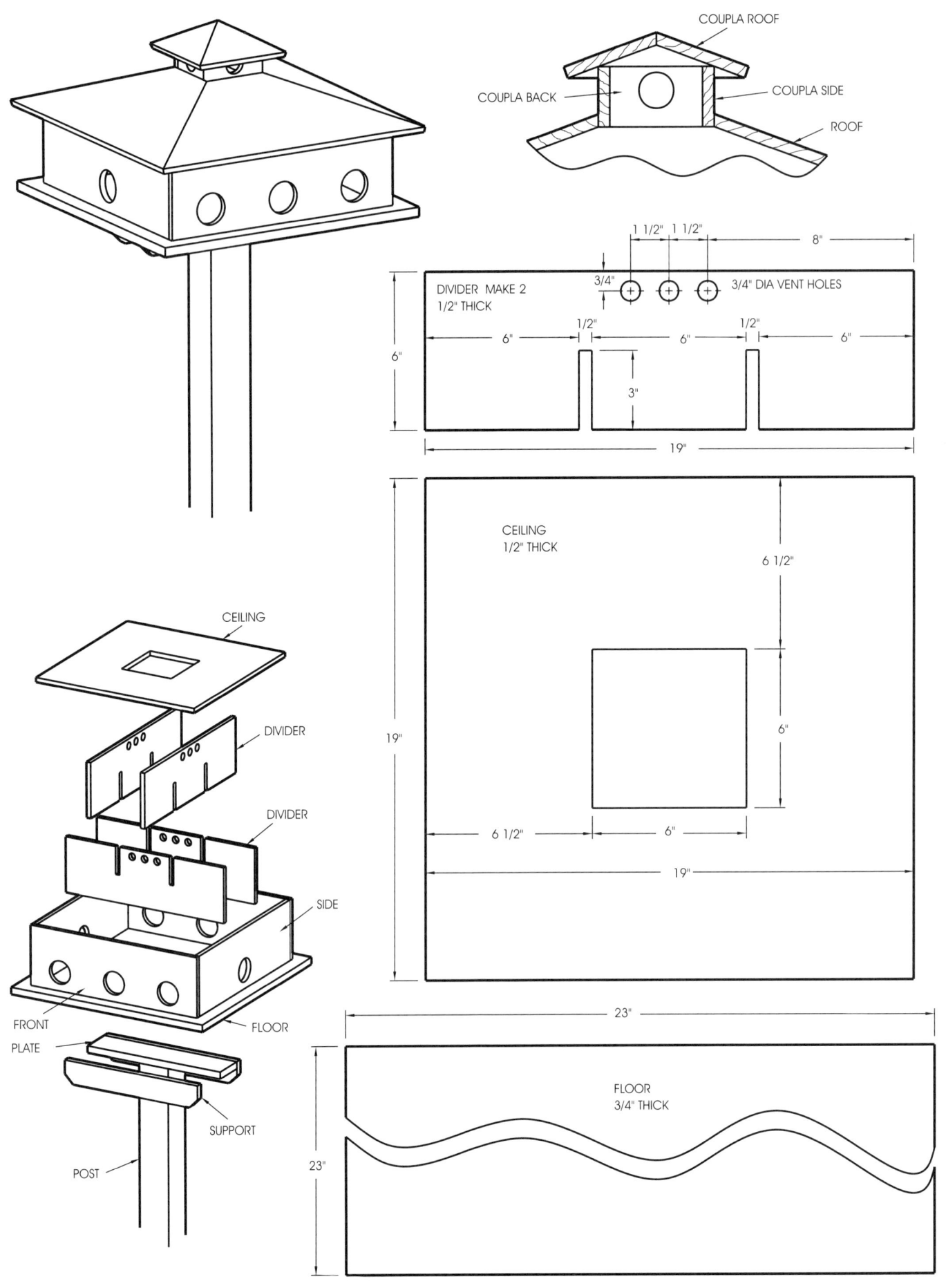

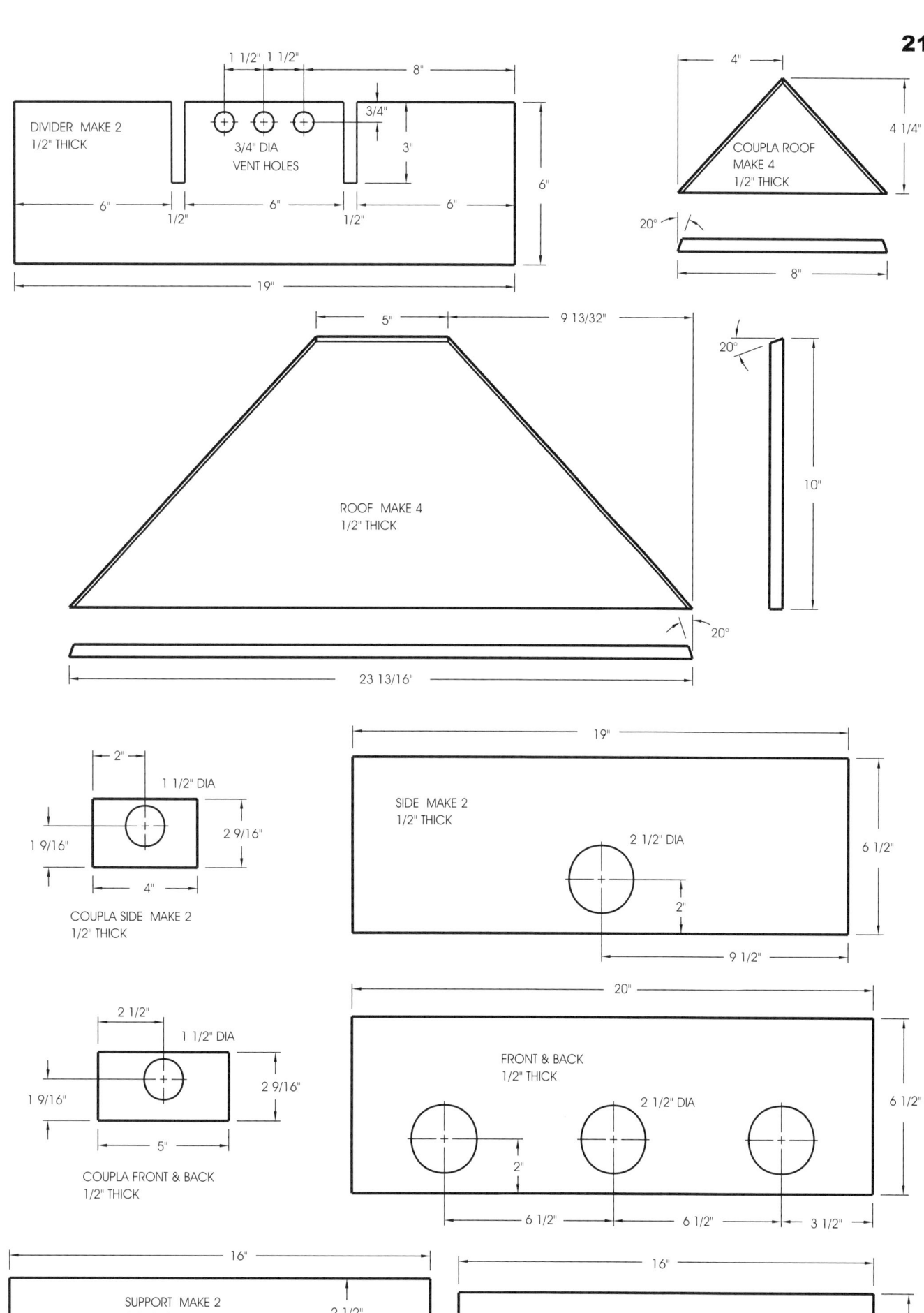

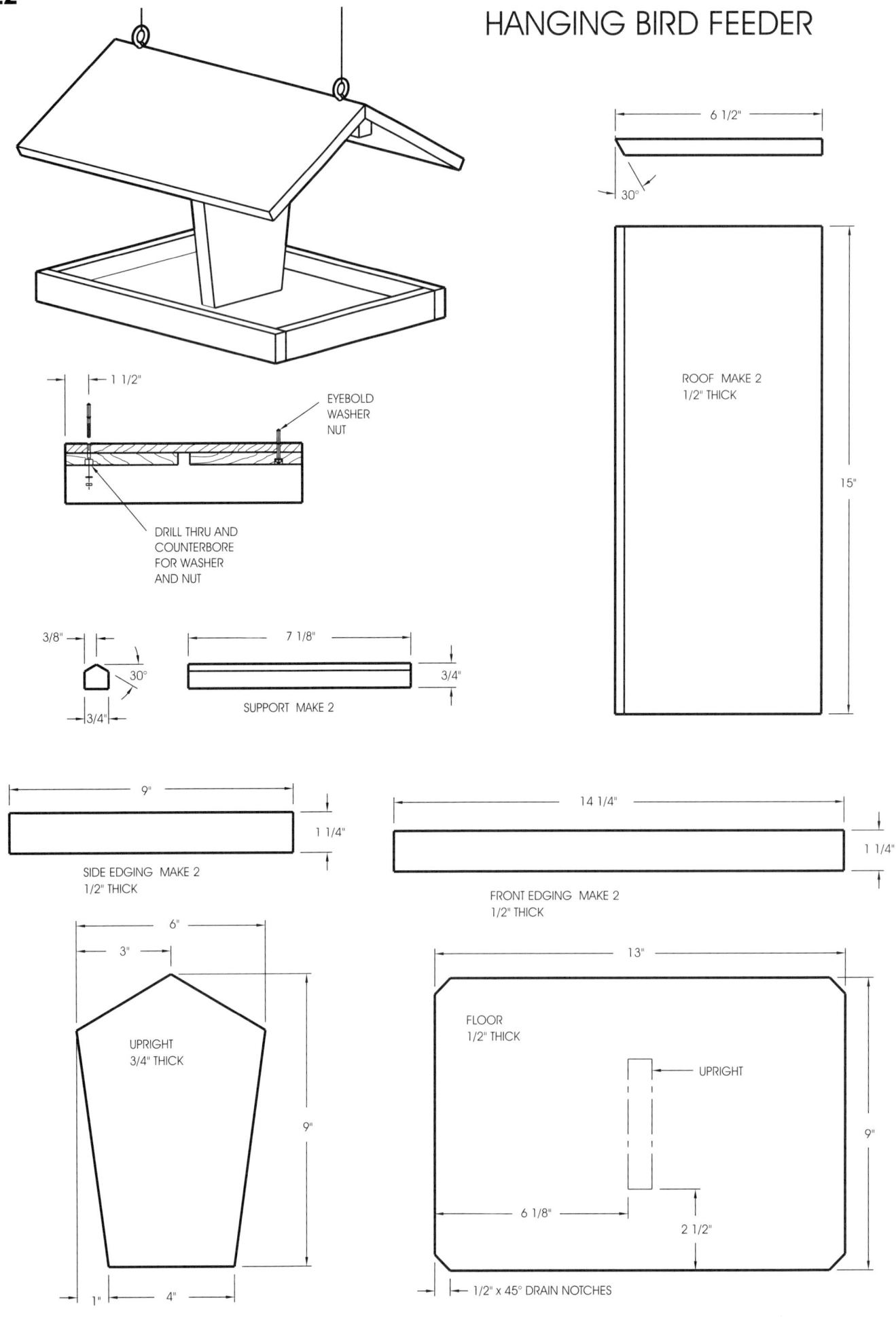

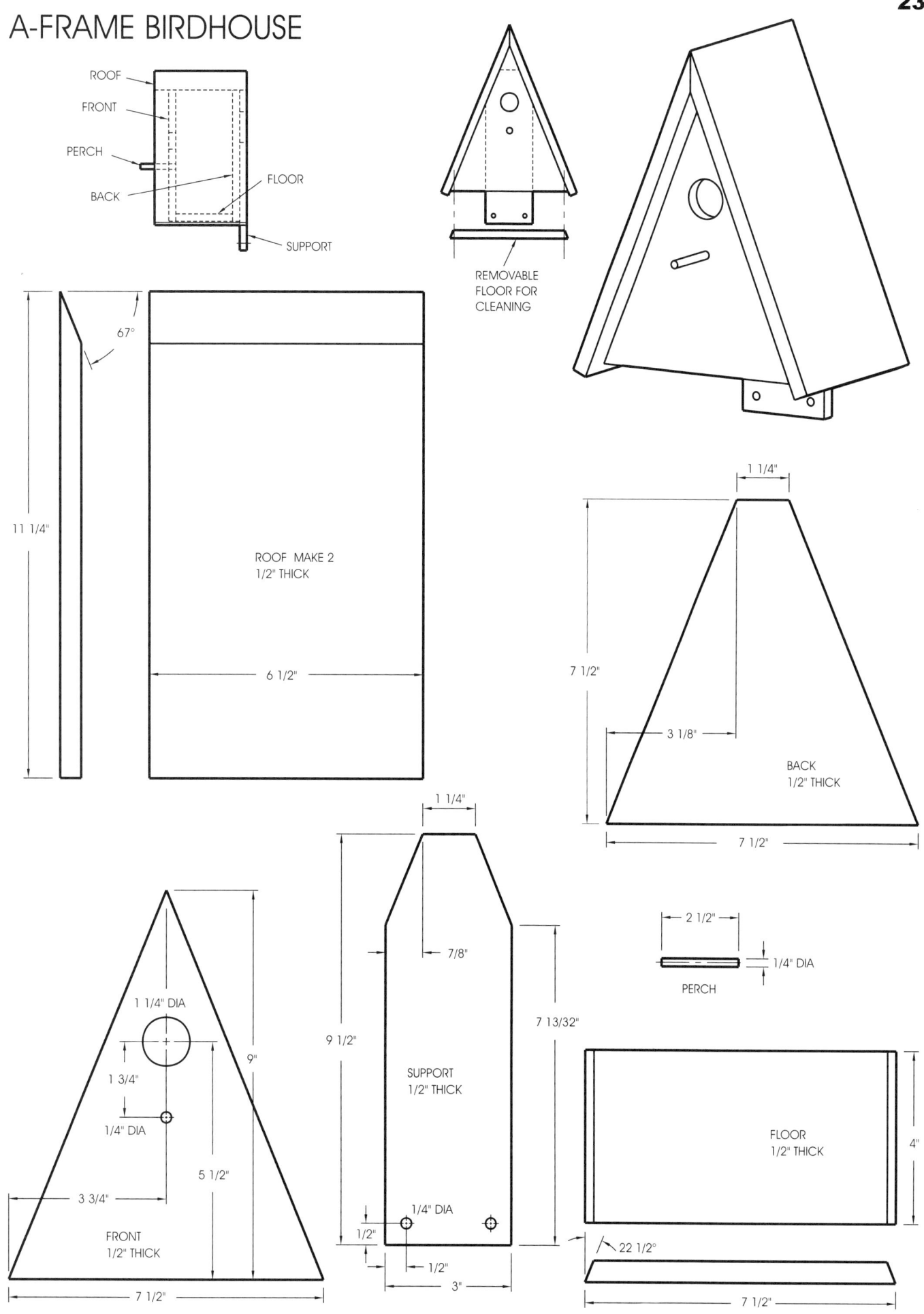

SCHOOL HOUSE BIRDHOUSE

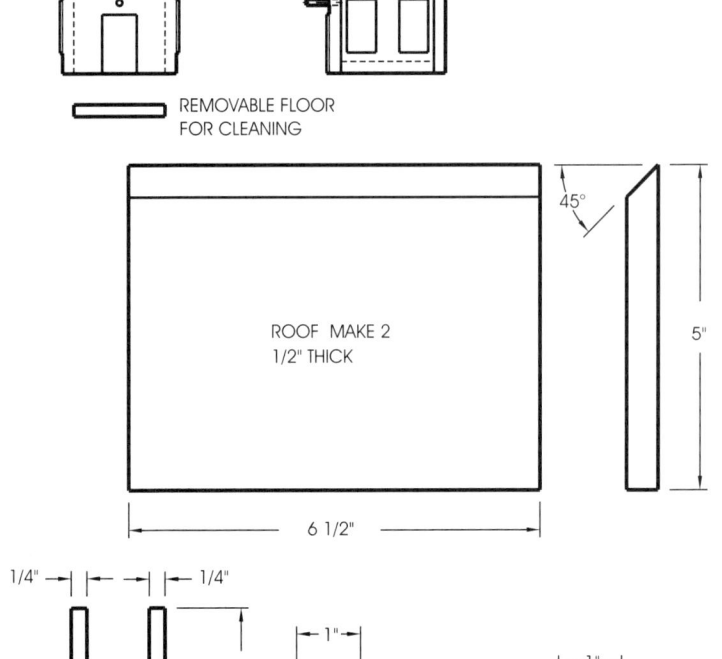

REMOVABLE FLOOR FOR CLEANING

ROOF MAKE 2
1/2" THICK

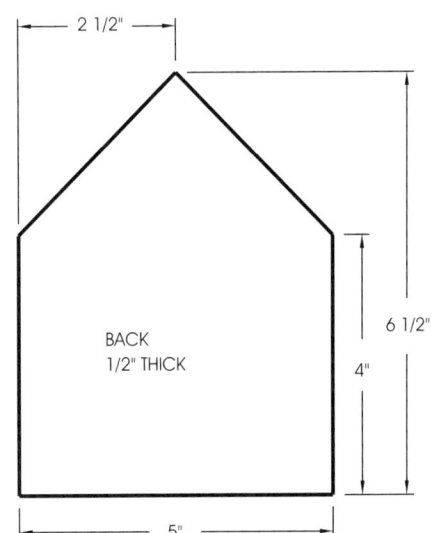

BACK
1/2" THICK

COUPLA FRONT
MAKE 2
1/4" THICK

COUPLA SIDE
MAKE 2
1/4" THICK

COUPLA ROOF
SQUARE

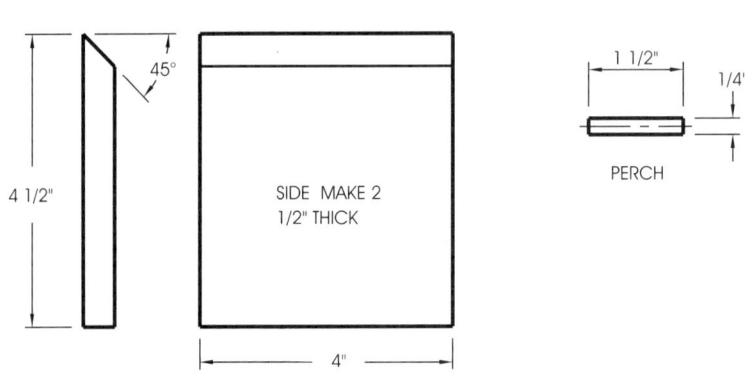

SIDE MAKE 2
1/2" THICK

PERCH
1/4" DIA

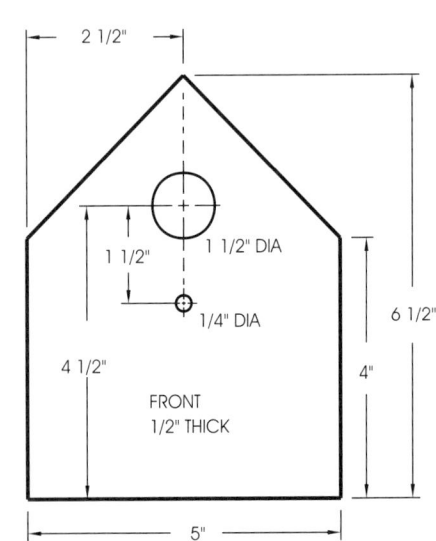

FRONT
1/2" THICK

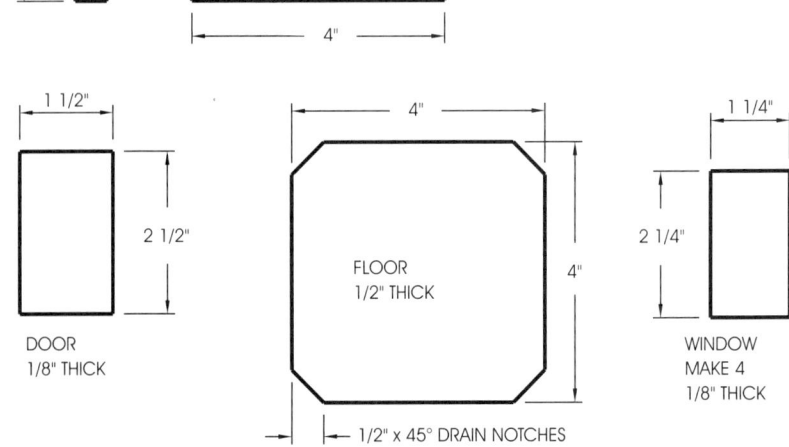

DOOR
1/8" THICK

FLOOR
1/2" THICK

1/2" x 45° DRAIN NOTCHES

WINDOW
MAKE 4
1/8" THICK

DOVE COVE

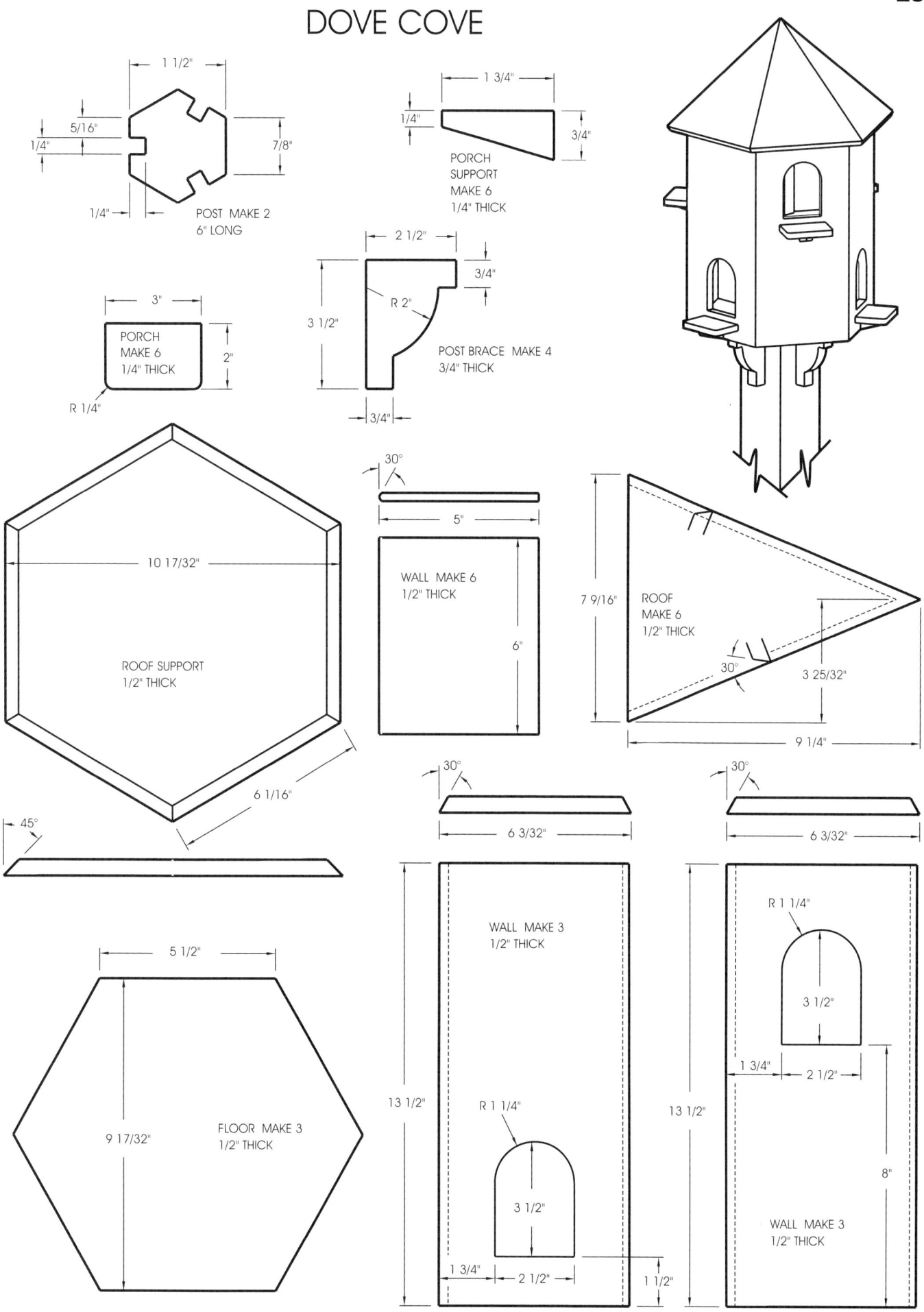

CHURCH BIRDHOUSE

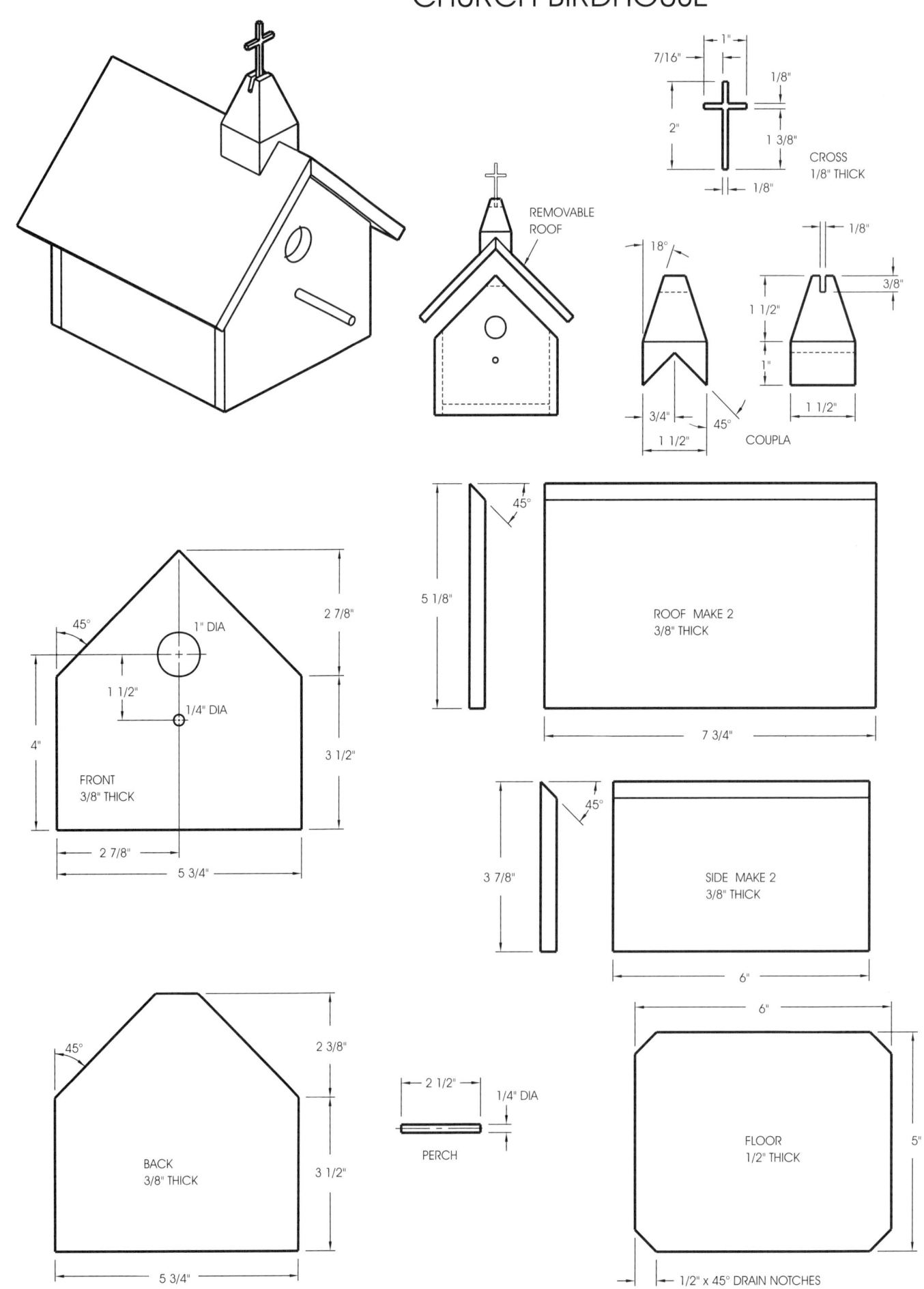

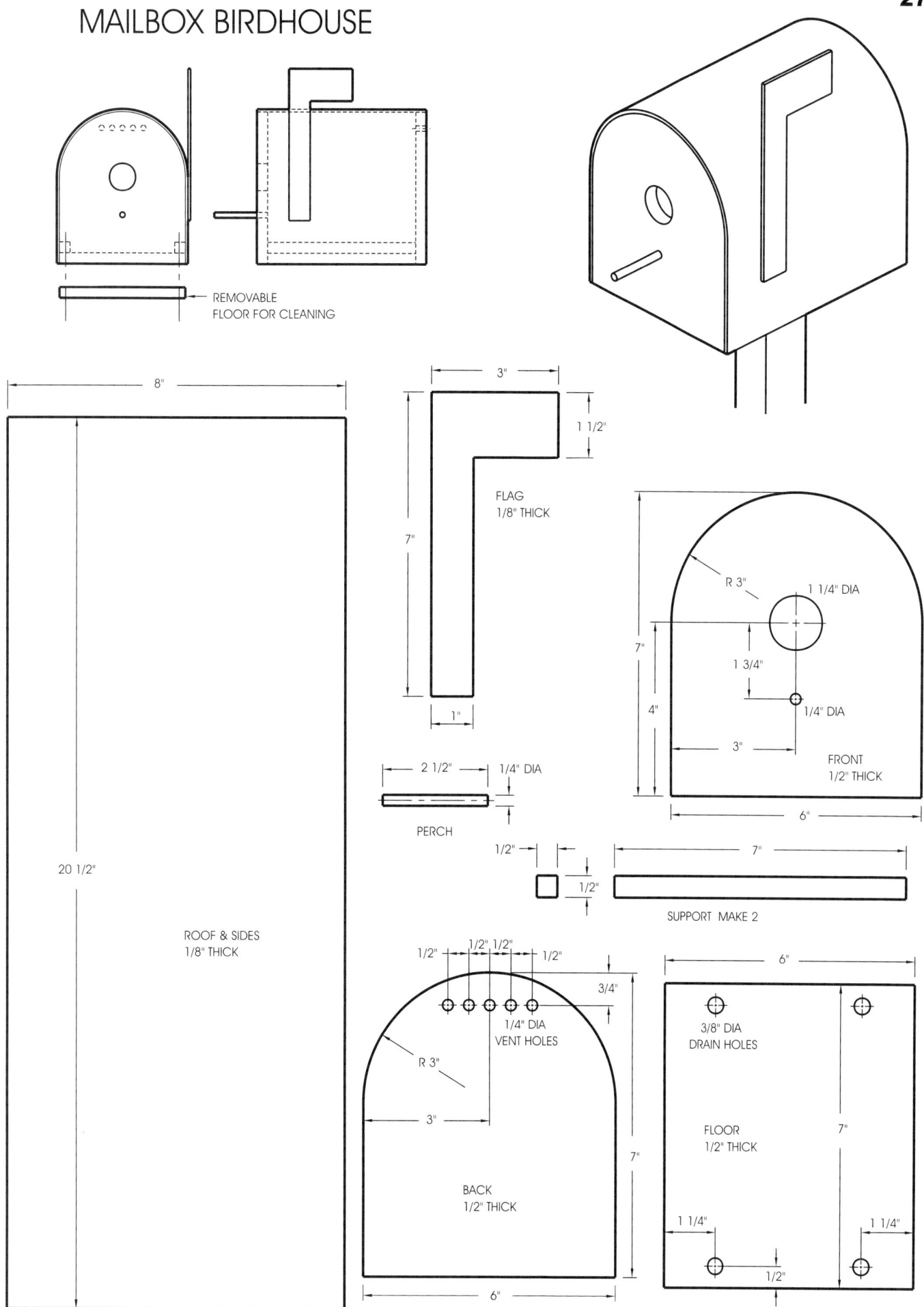

16-APARTMENT MARTIN BIRDHOUSE

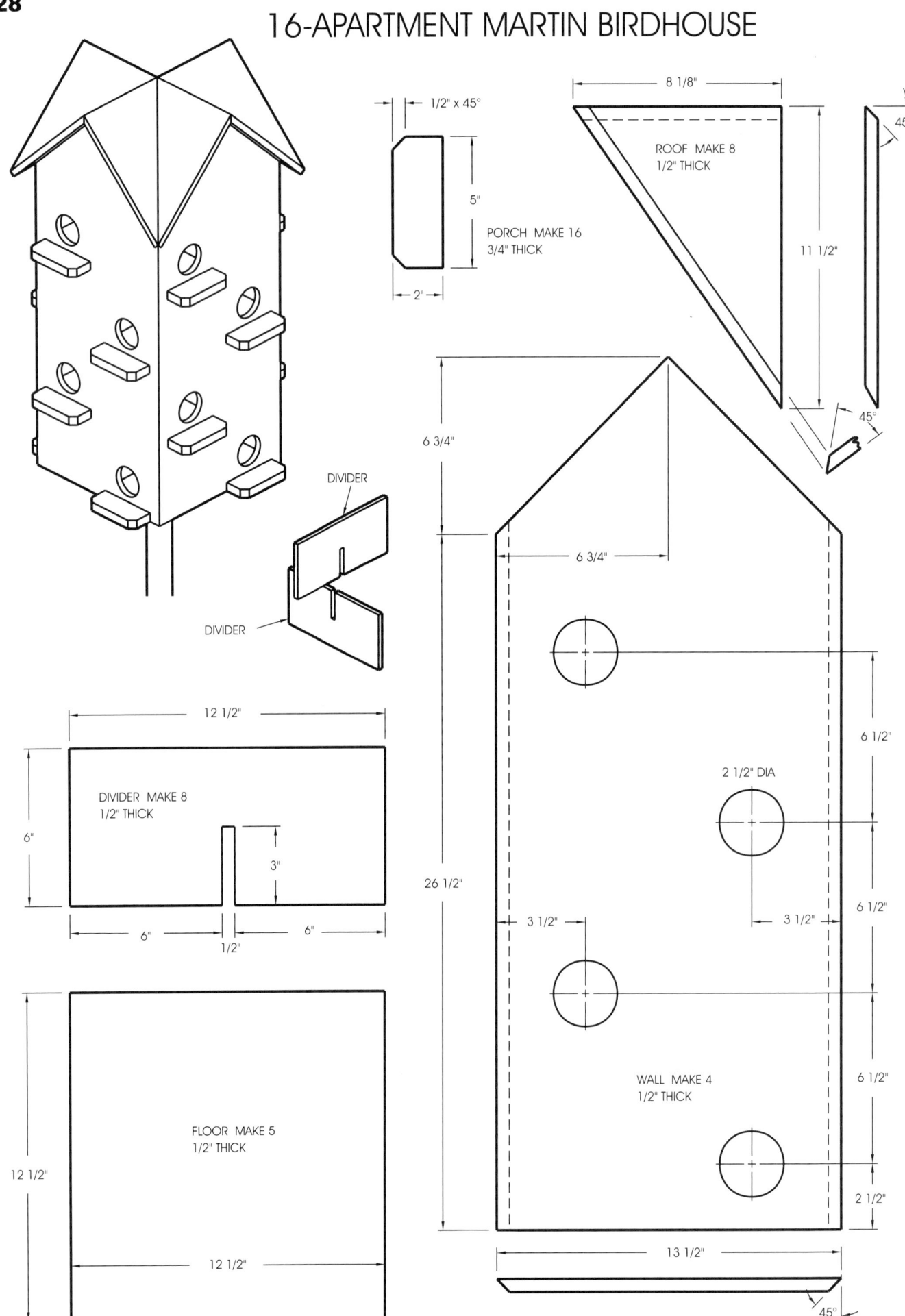

FARM HOUSE BIRDHOUSE

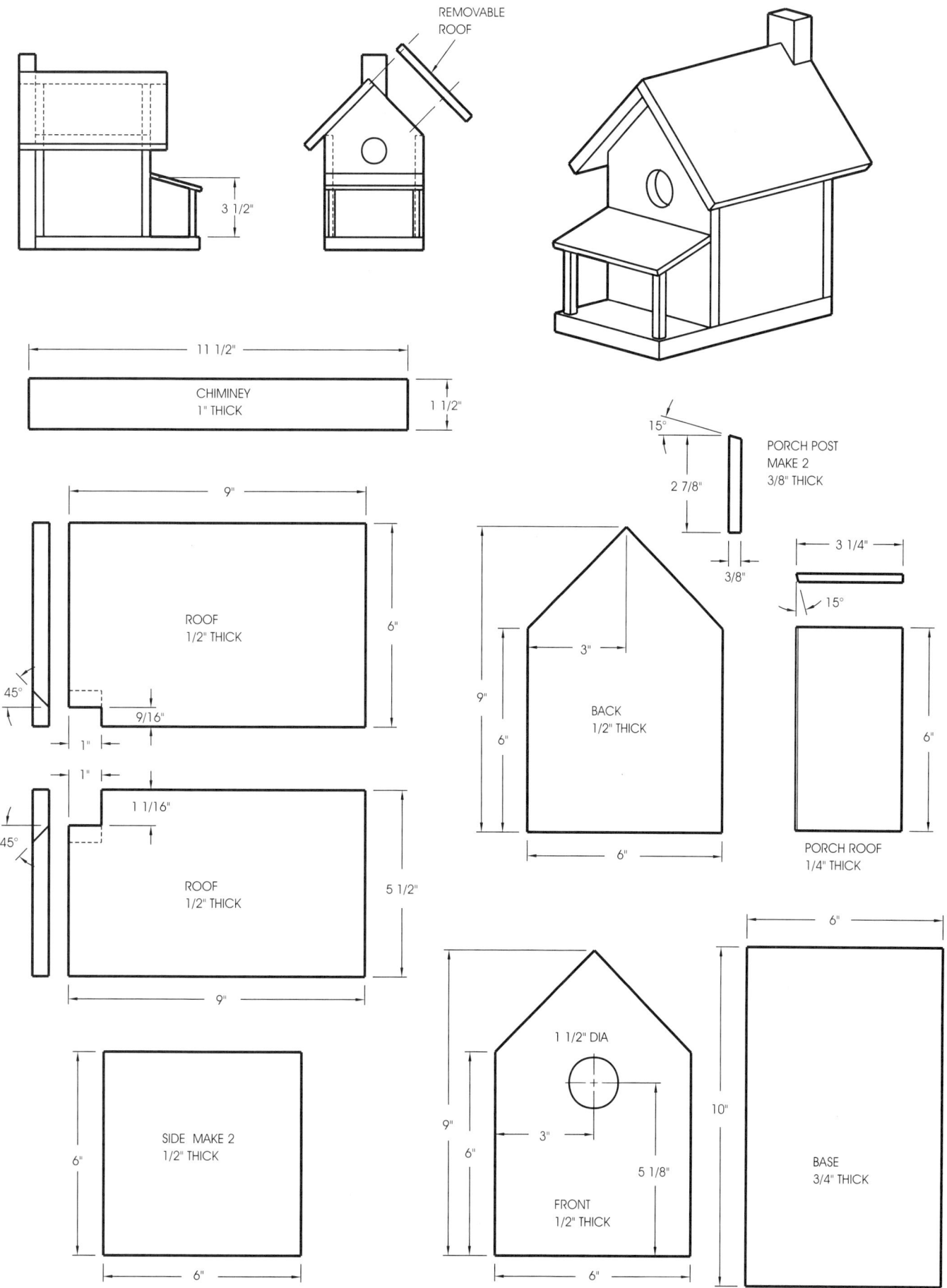

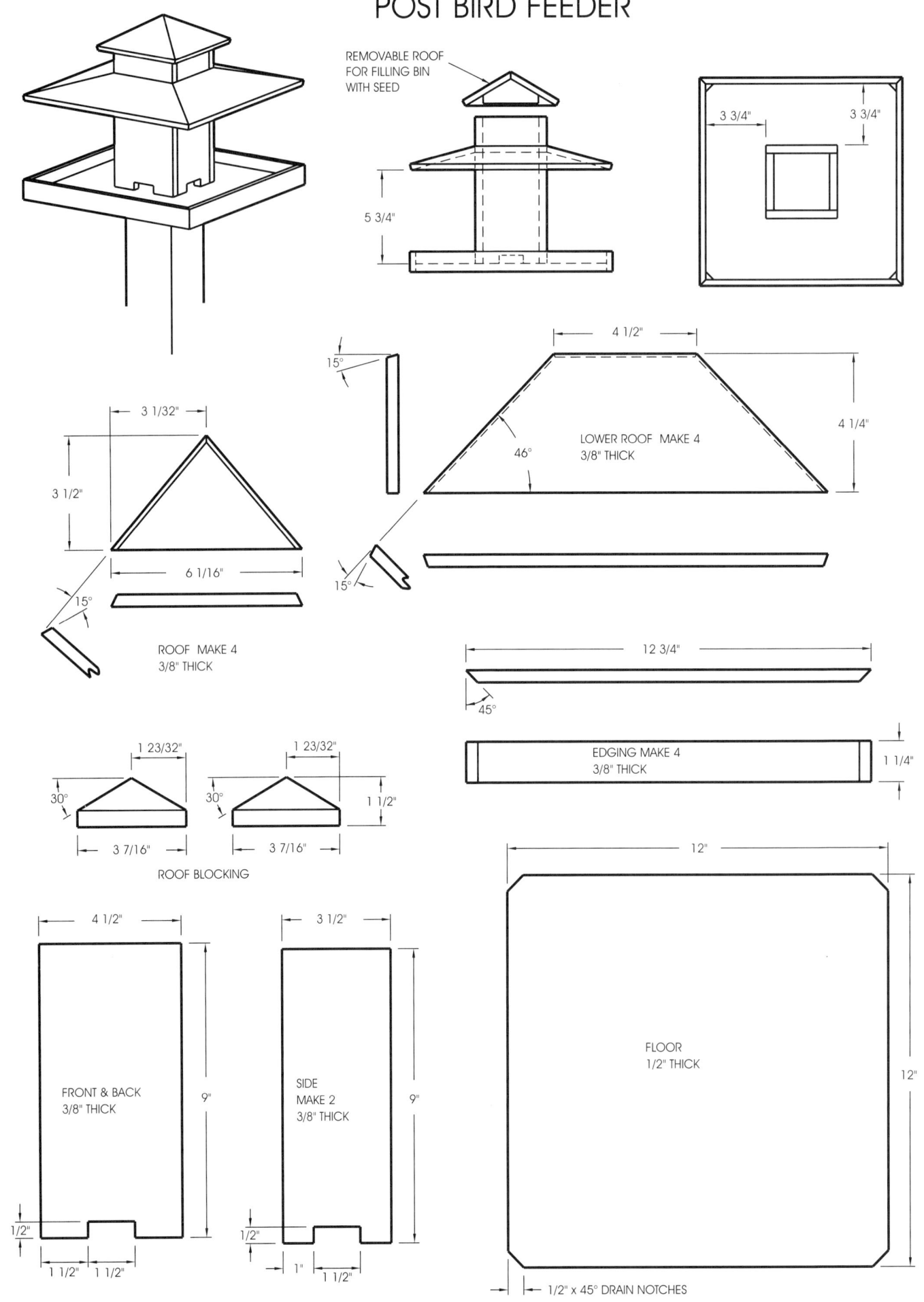

HOPPER BIRD FEEDER

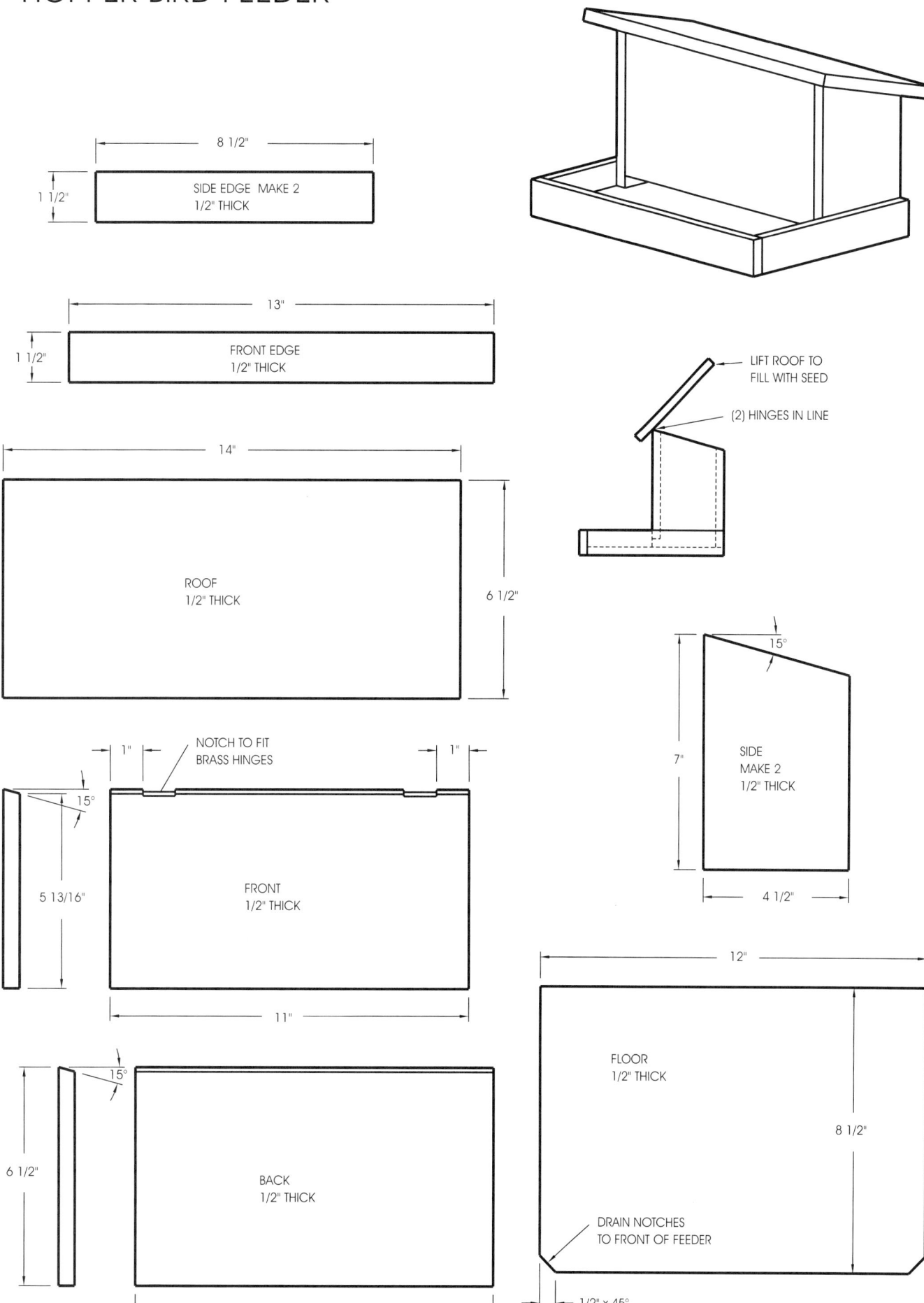

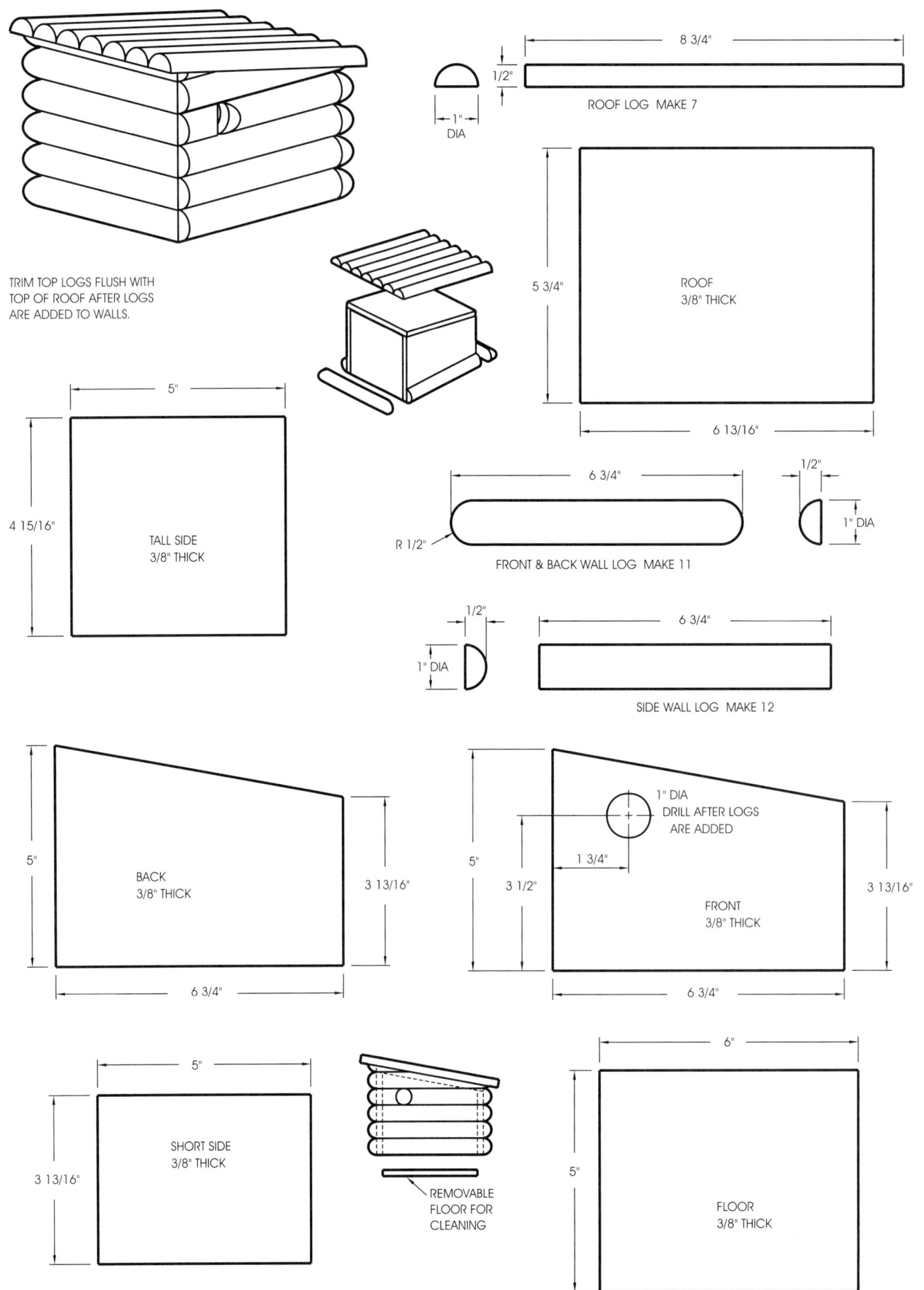

BIRDHOUSE FOR TREE SWALLOWS

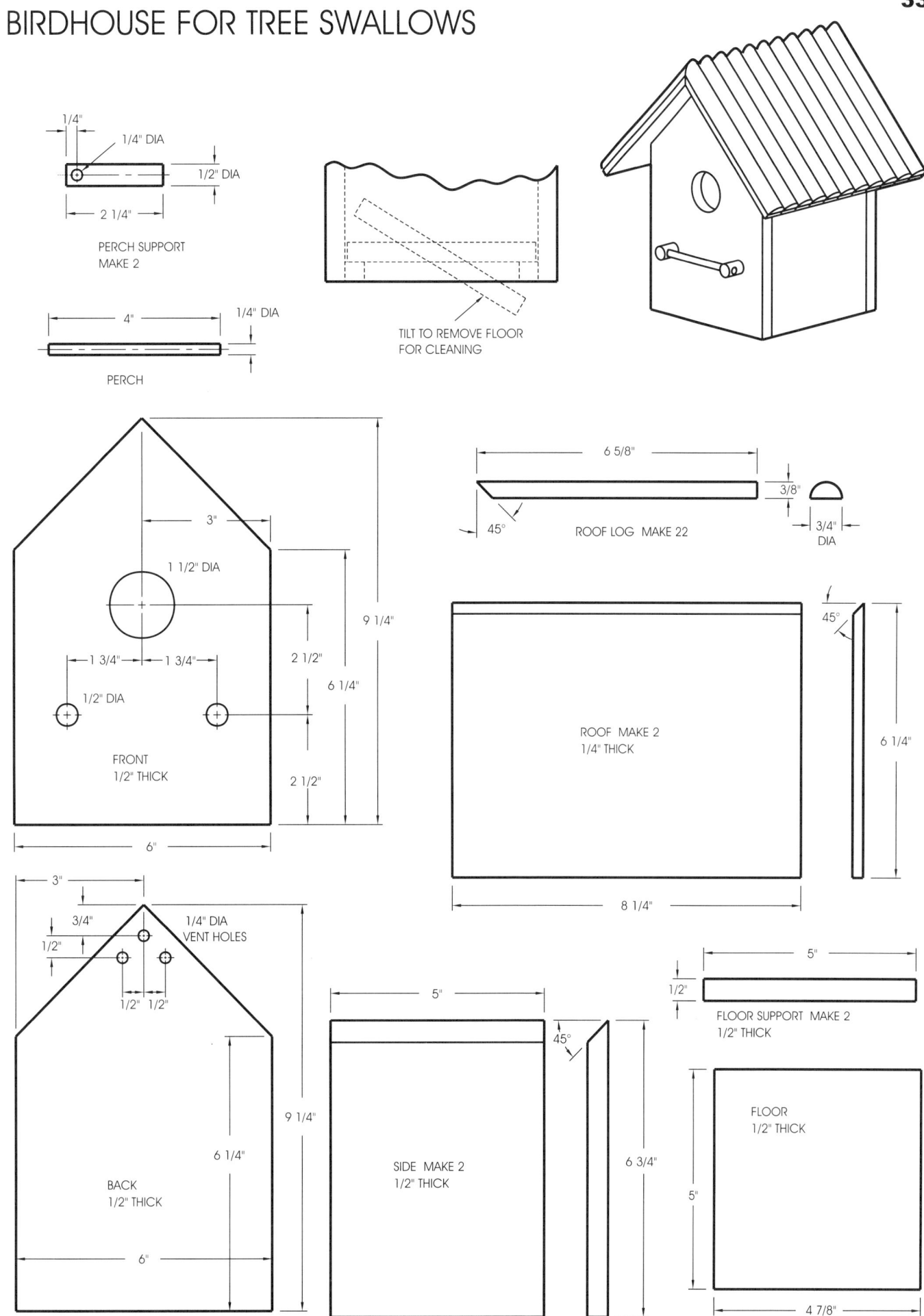

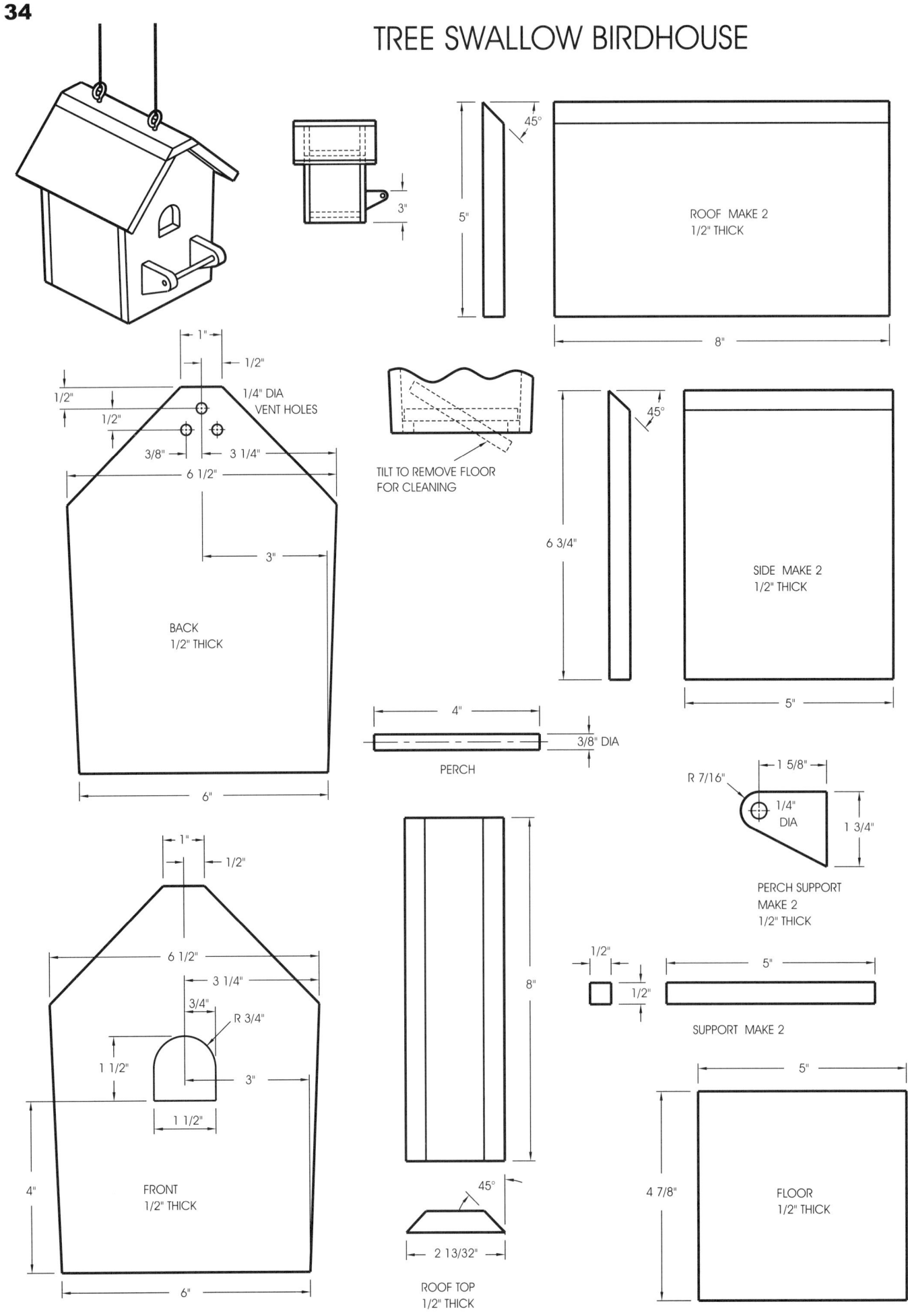

ROBIN NESTING SHELF

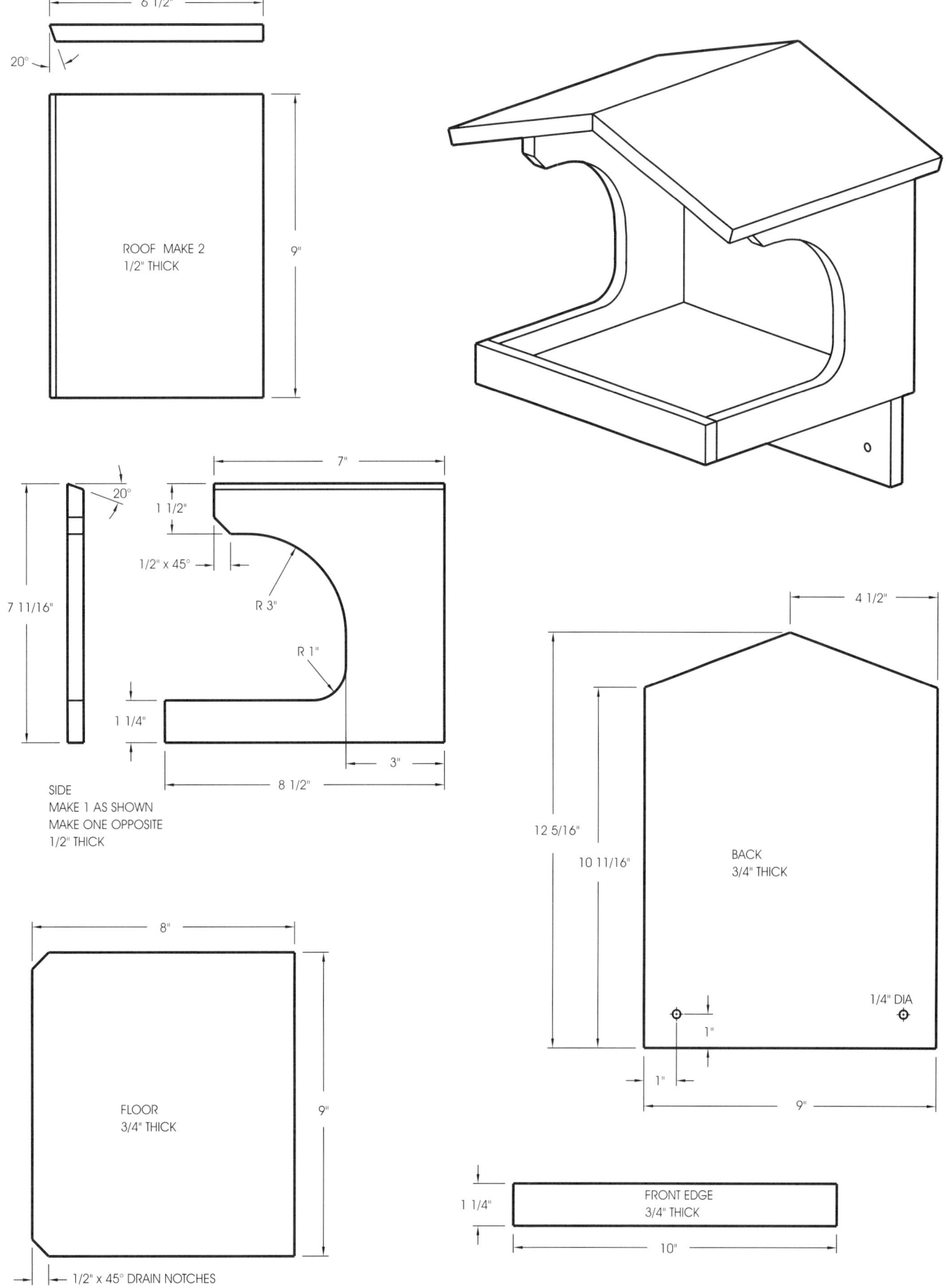

LOG HOUSE BIRDHOUSE

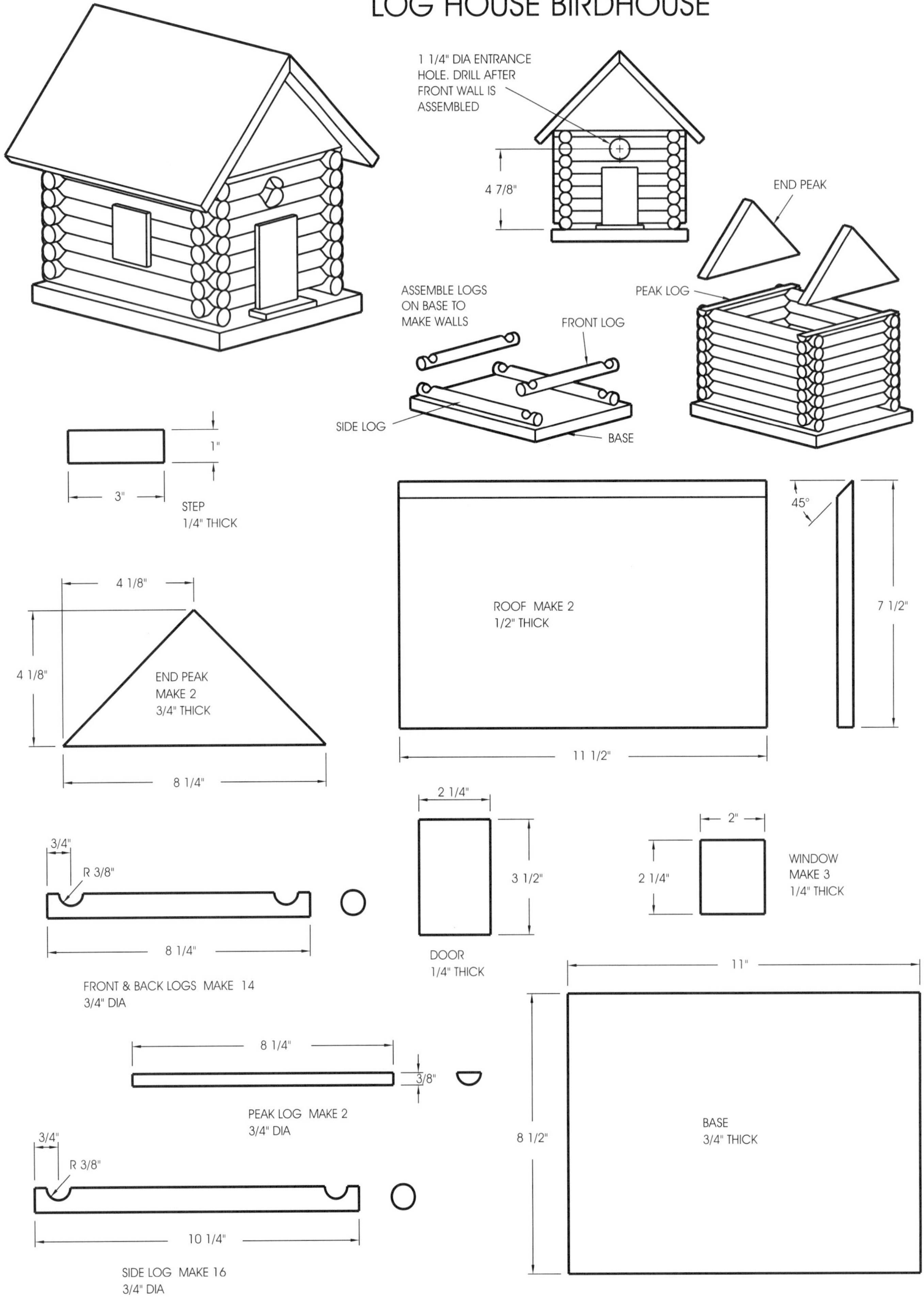

1 1/4" DIA ENTRANCE HOLE. DRILL AFTER FRONT WALL IS ASSEMBLED

4 7/8"

END PEAK

ASSEMBLE LOGS ON BASE TO MAKE WALLS

FRONT LOG

SIDE LOG

BASE

PEAK LOG

STEP
1" × 3"
1/4" THICK

45°

7 1/2"

ROOF MAKE 2
1/2" THICK

11 1/2"

END PEAK MAKE 2
3/4" THICK
4 1/8" × 4 1/8" × 8 1/4"

2 1/4" × 3 1/2"
DOOR
1/4" THICK

2" × 2 1/4"
WINDOW MAKE 3
1/4" THICK

FRONT & BACK LOGS MAKE 14
3/4" DIA
3/4", R 3/8", 8 1/4"

PEAK LOG MAKE 2
3/4" DIA
8 1/4", 3/8"

SIDE LOG MAKE 16
3/4" DIA
3/4", R 3/8", 10 1/4"

BASE
3/4" THICK
11" × 8 1/2"

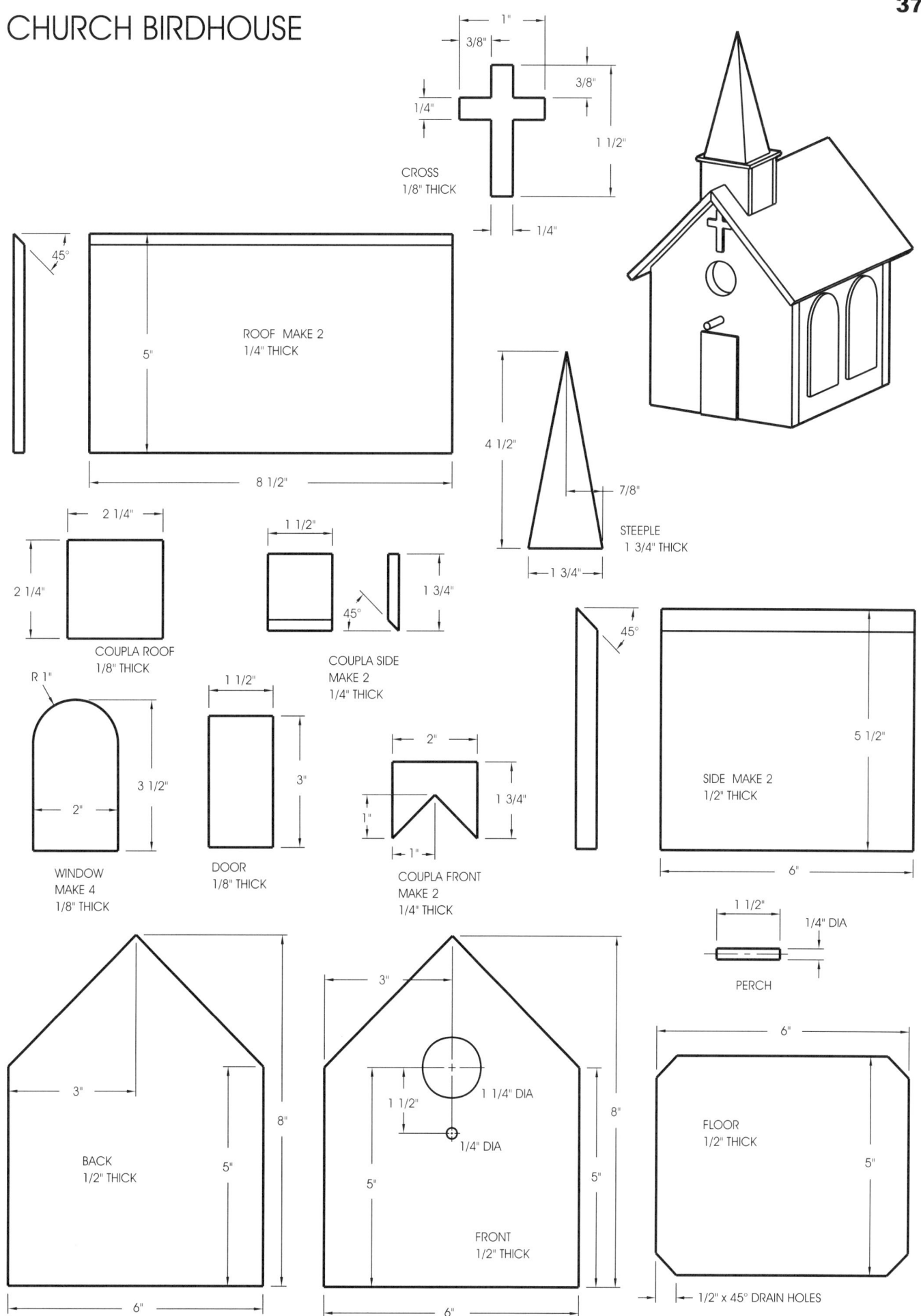

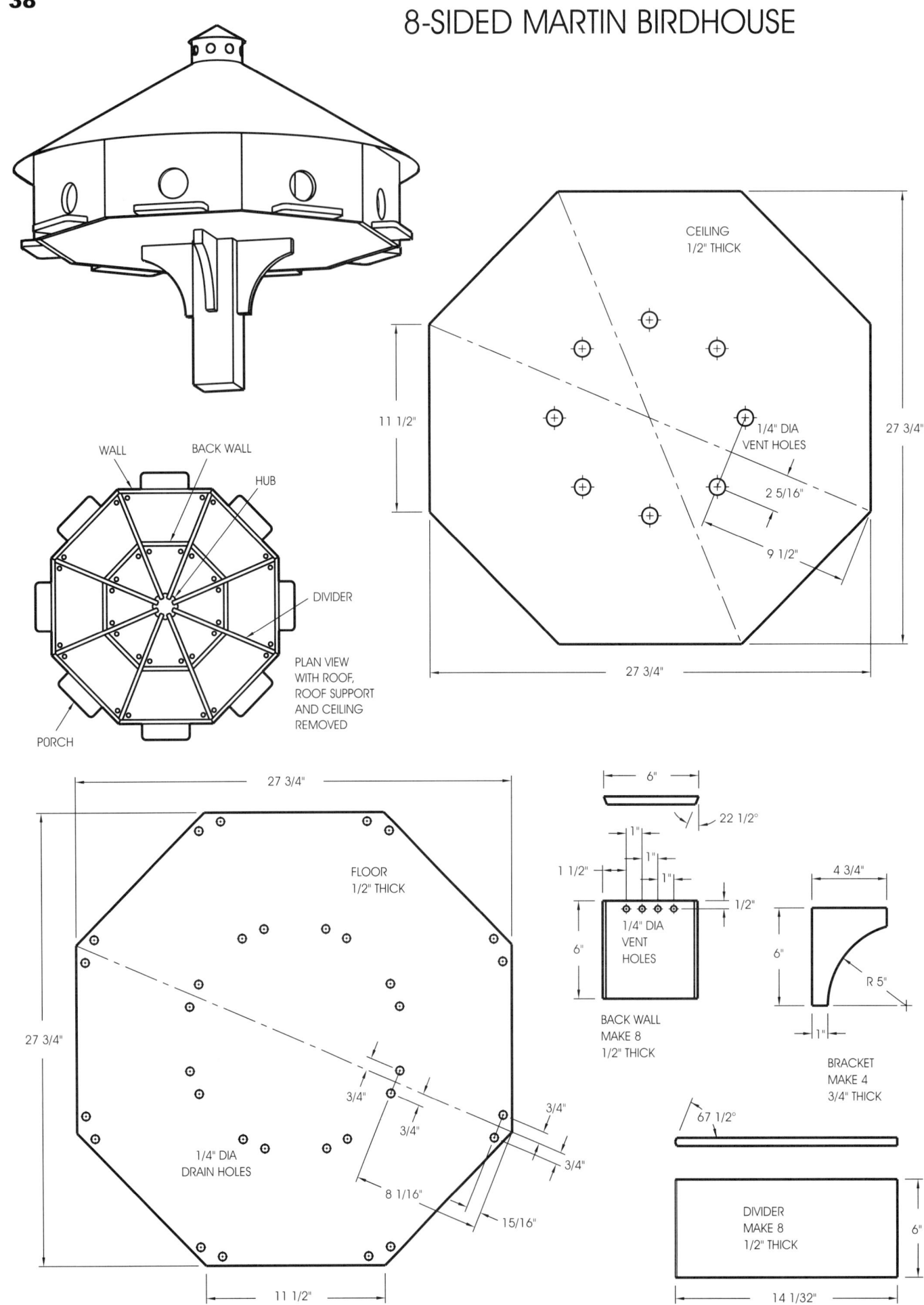

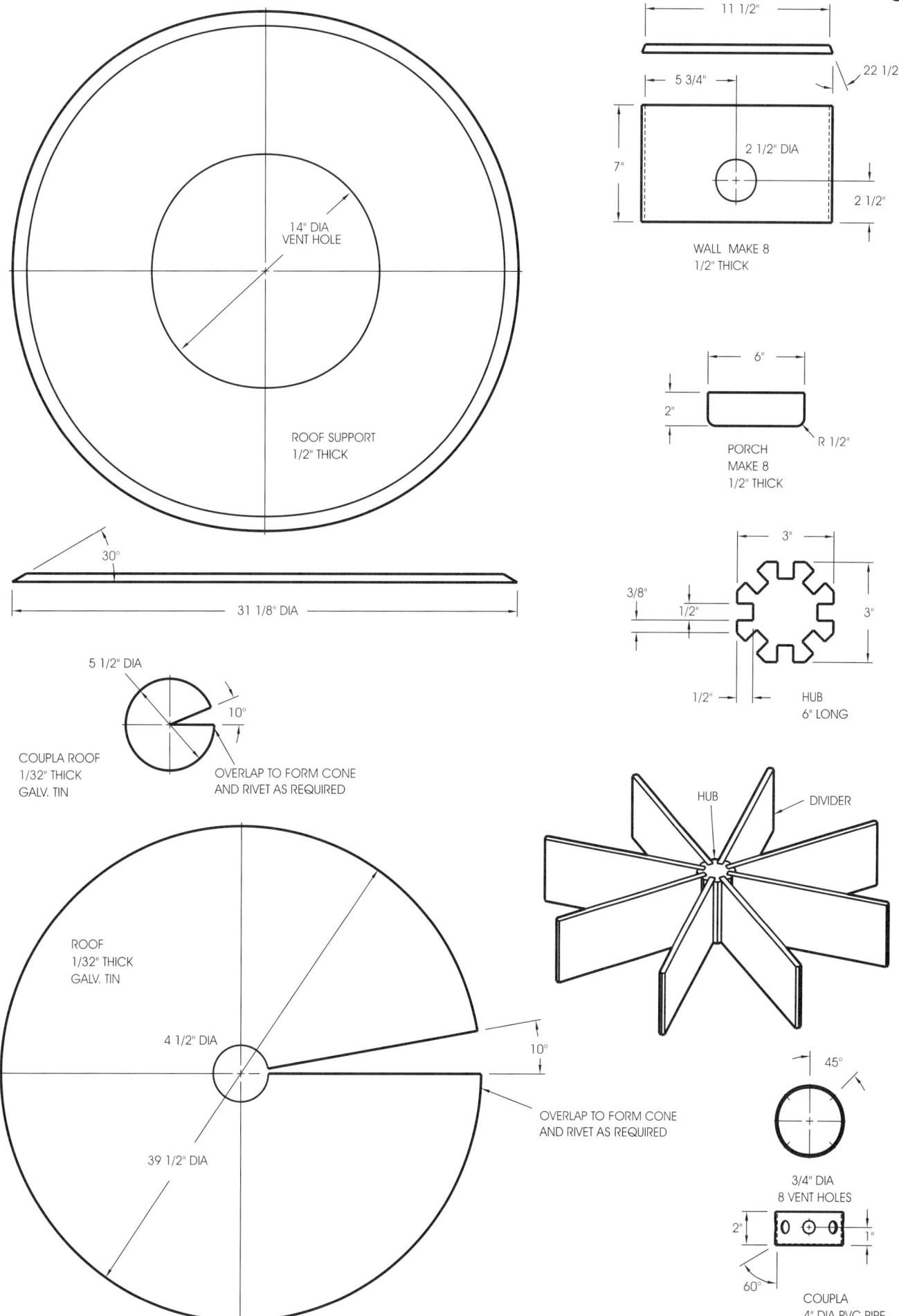

TRIANGLE DOVE COVE

PORCH SUPPORT
MAKE 6
3/8" THICK

- 1 1/2"
- 3/4"
- R 3/4"

- 6"
- 3/8"
- 6"
- 6"

ROOF
MAKE 2
1/2" THICK

- 63°
- 30 1/2"
- 9"

CEILING
1/2" THICK
- 6"
- 6"
- 26°

PORCH 3
3/8" THICK
- 4"
- 2"
- 1" x 45°

PORCH 2
3/8" THICK
- 10 1/2"
- 2"
- 1" x 45°

PORCH 1
3/8" THICK
- 17"
- 2"
- 1" x 45°

FLOOR 3
1/2" THICK
- 6"
- 12 1/2"
- 26°

WALL
MAKE 3
1/2" THICK
- 6"
- 6"

FLOOR 2
1/2" THICK
- 6"
- 19"
- 26°

FLOOR 1
1/2" THICK
- 6"
- 25 1/2"
- 26°

FRONT & BACK
1/2" THICK
ENTRY OPENINGS
IN FRONT ONLY

- 25 1/2"
- 3 1/2"
- R 1 1/4"
- 6 1/2"
- 2 1/2"
- 3 1/4"
- 3 1/4"
- 3 1/2"
- 6 1/2"
- 1 1/2"
- 6 1/2"
- 6 1/2"
- 12 3/4"
- 25 1/2"

ADOBE BIRDHOUSE

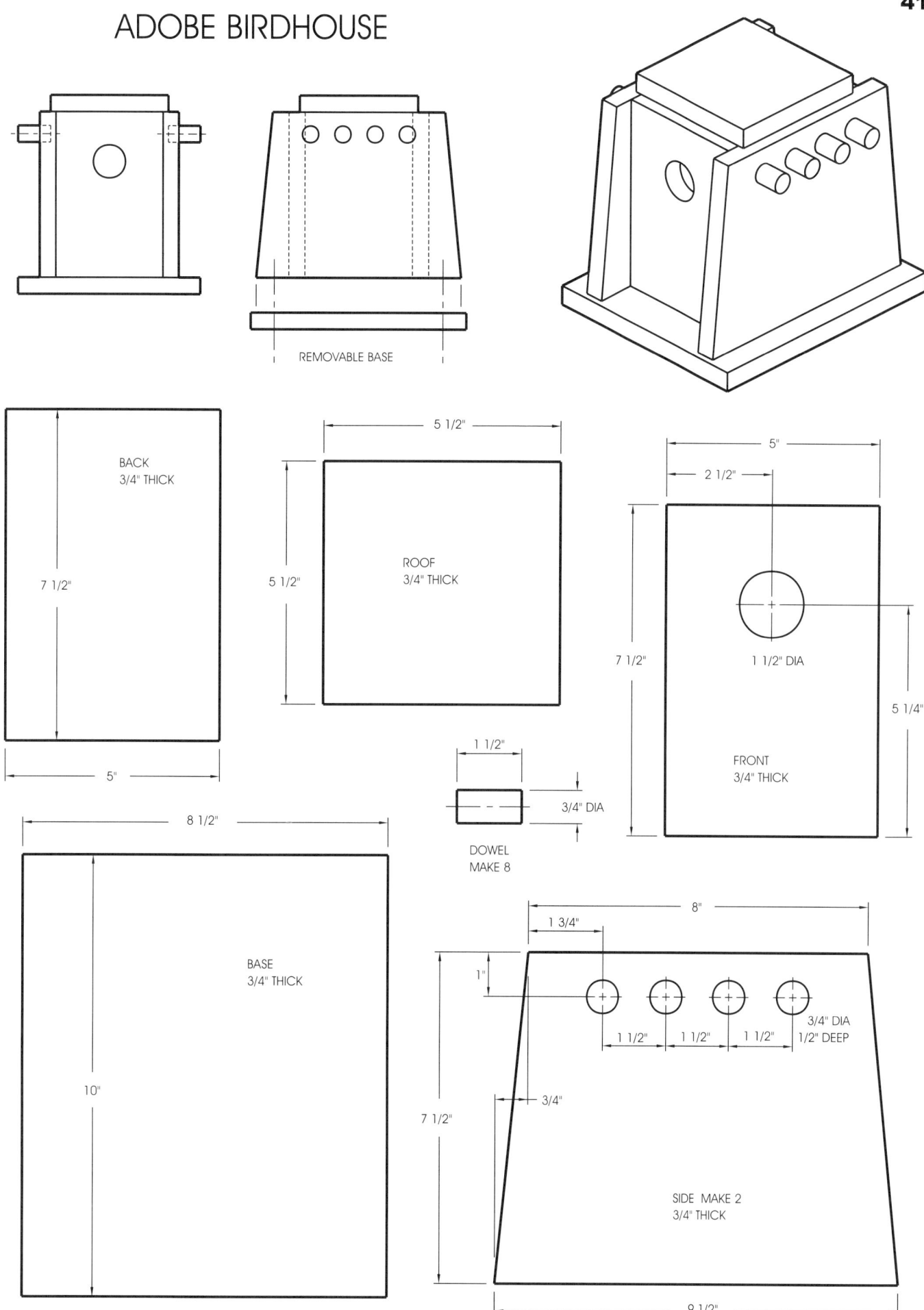

TWO DWELLING BIRDHOUSE

PORCH 3/4" THICK
- 8 1/2"
- 2"
- 1" x 45°

BASE 3/4" THICK
- 9"
- 10"
- 1" x 45°

BACK TRIM 3/4" THICK
- 3/4"
- 8 1/2"

SIDE TRIM MAKE 2 3/4" THICK
- 3/4"
- 7"

- 5 3/4"

FLOOR 1/2" THICK
- 6" x 6"

ROOF MAKE 2 1/2" THICK
- 9"
- 6 3/4"
- 45°

BACK 1/2" THICK
- 3 1/2"
- 14 1/2"
- 11"
- 7"

FRONT 1/2" THICK
- 3 1/2"
- 2 1/2" DIA
- 14 1/2"
- 11"
- 6 1/2"
- 7"
- 2"

SIDE MAKE 2 1/2" THICK
- 6"
- 11"
- 45°

NESTING SHELF

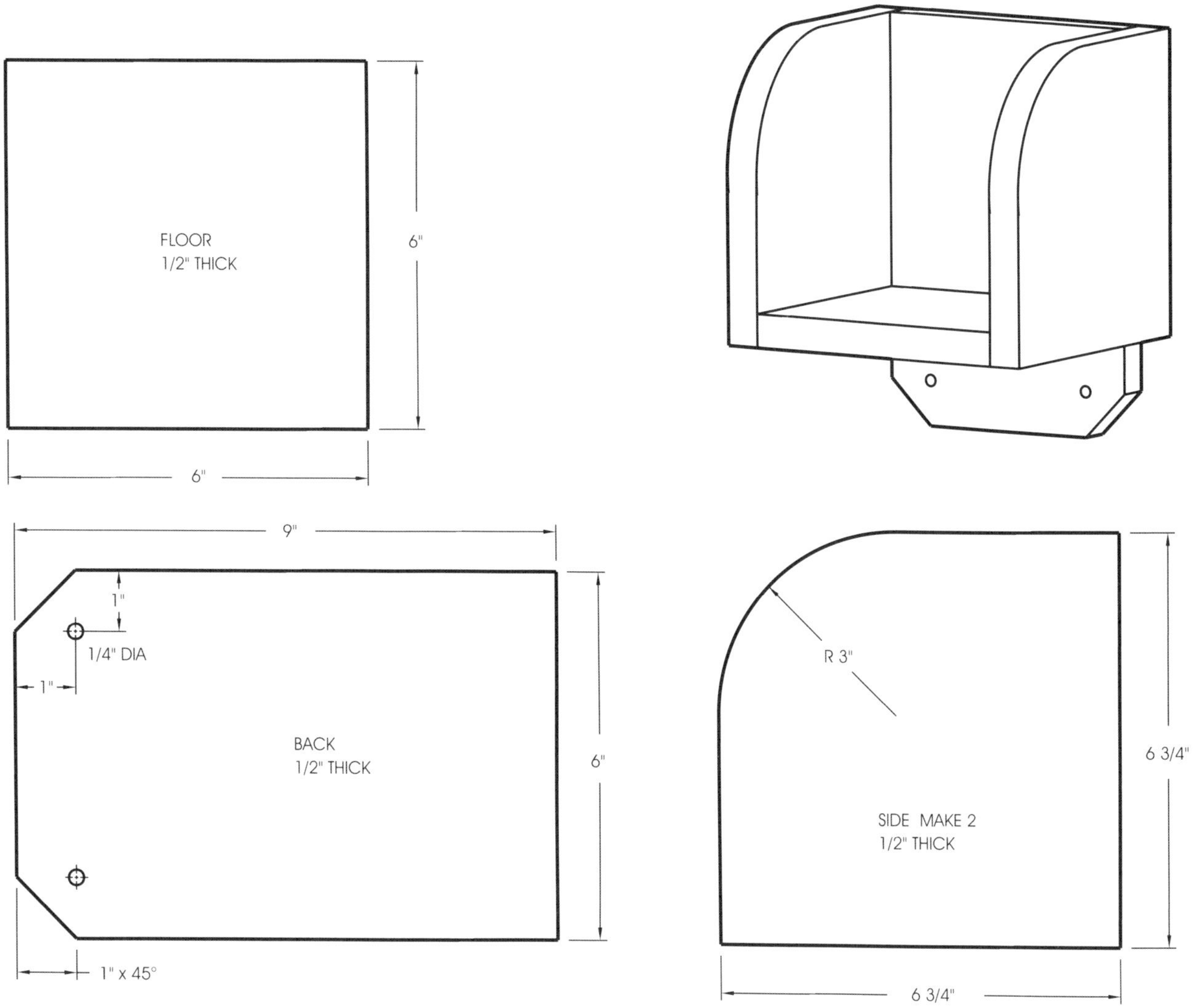

BIRD FEEDING TABLE

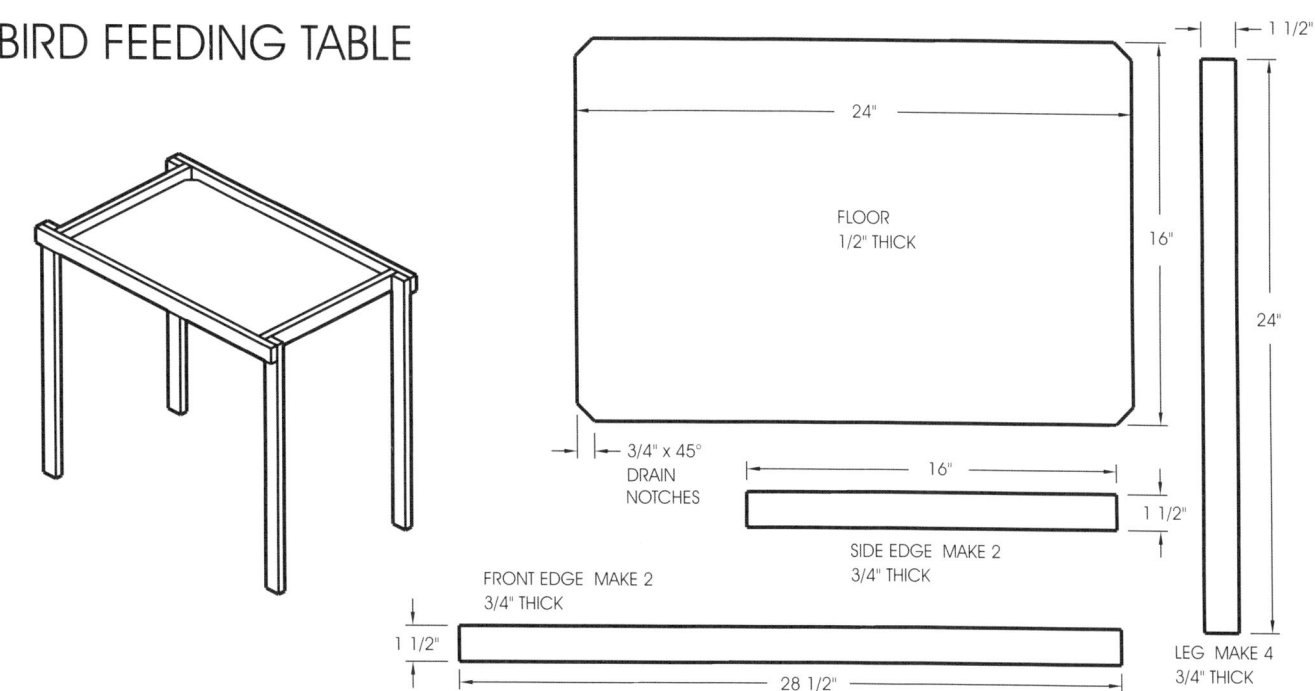

18-APARTMENT MARTIN BIRDHOUSE

DIVIDER
DIVIDER 3
FRONT 3
FLOOR 3
SIDE 3

DIVIDER
DIVIDER 1
BACK 1
SIDE 1
FRONT 1
FLOOR 1
SUPPORT

FRONT 3 & BACK 3
1/2" THICK
- 15°
- 11 1/4"
- 1 1/2" DIA
- 1 1/2"
- 2"
- 7 3/4"
- 7 3/4"
- 11 1/4"
- 22 1/2"

SIDE 3 MAKE 2
1/2" THICK
- 13 1/2"
- 1 17/32"
- 25°
- 15°

FRONT 2 & BACK 2
1/2" THICK
- 15°
- 1 1/2" DIA
- 6"
- 2"
- 9 1/2"
- 19"

SIDE 2 MAKE 2
1/2" THICK
- 13 1/2"
- 15°
- 6 11/32"
- 1 1/2" DIA
- 2"
- 3 1/2"
- 3 1/2"

FRONT 1 & BACK 1
1/2" THICK
- 15°
- 1 1/2" DIA
- 6"
- 2"
- 3"
- 3"
- 15 1/2"

SIDE 1 MAKE 2
1/2" THICK
- 15°
- 6 11/32"
- 13 1/2"

SUPPORT MAKE 2
3/4" THICK
- 12"
- 1"
- 3 1/2"
- 4 1/4"
- 3 1/2"

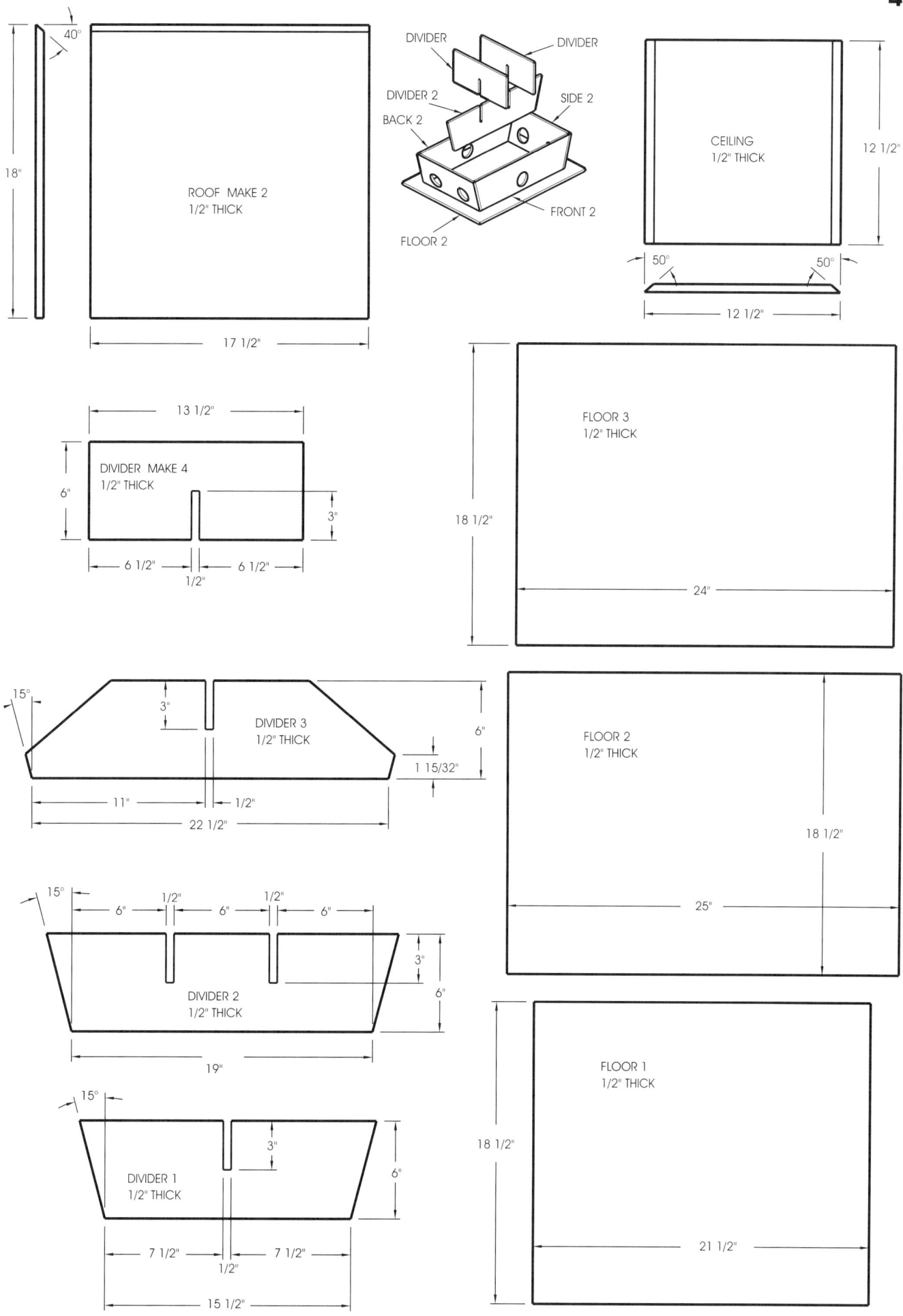

FOUR POST BIRD FEEDER

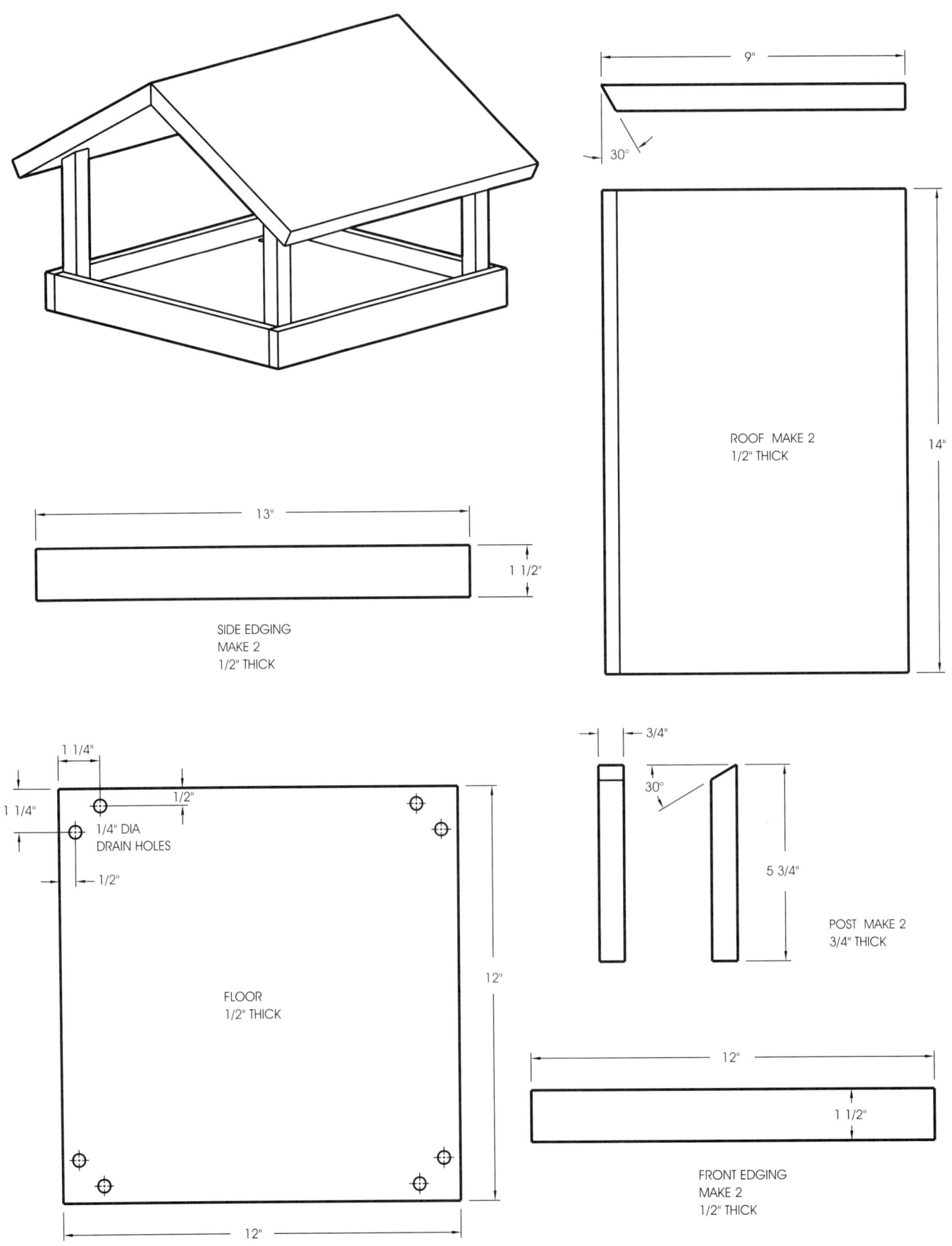

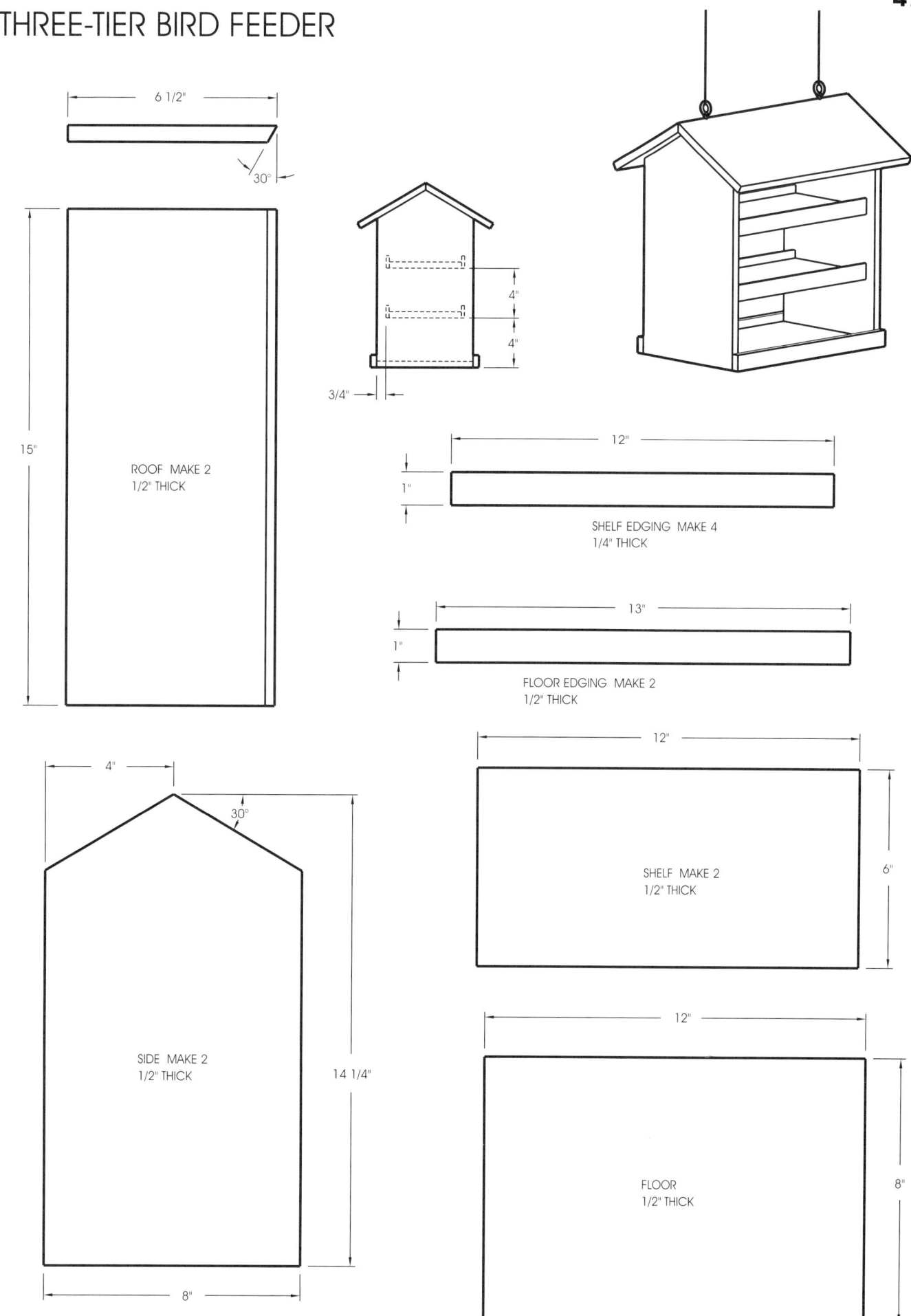

SLAB LOG CABIN BIRDHOUSE

ROOF MAKE 2
1/2" THICK
9"
5 3/4"
45°

FRONT
1/2" THICK
6"
3"
1/8"
1 1/4" DIA
1 1/4"
1/4" DIA
7 1/2"
4 1/2"
1/2"
1/2"
5/8"
6 1/4"
5/8"
SCRIBE LINES WITH AN AWL AND STRAIGHT EDGE

WALLS INTERLOCK AT CORNERS TO FORM EXPOSED END DETAIL

DOOR
1/8" THICK
1 1/2"
3"

PERCH
2"
1/4" DIA

FLOOR
1/2" THICK
6"
5"
1/2" x 45° DRAIN NOTCHES

BACK
1/2" THICK
6"
3"
1/8"
7 1/2"
4 1/2"
1/2"
1/2"
5/8"
6 1/4"
5/8"

SIDE MAKE 2
1/2" THICK
7 1/4"
4 1/2"
1/2"
1/2"
5/8"
5/8"

MODERN HIGH-RISE BUILDING BIRDHOUSE

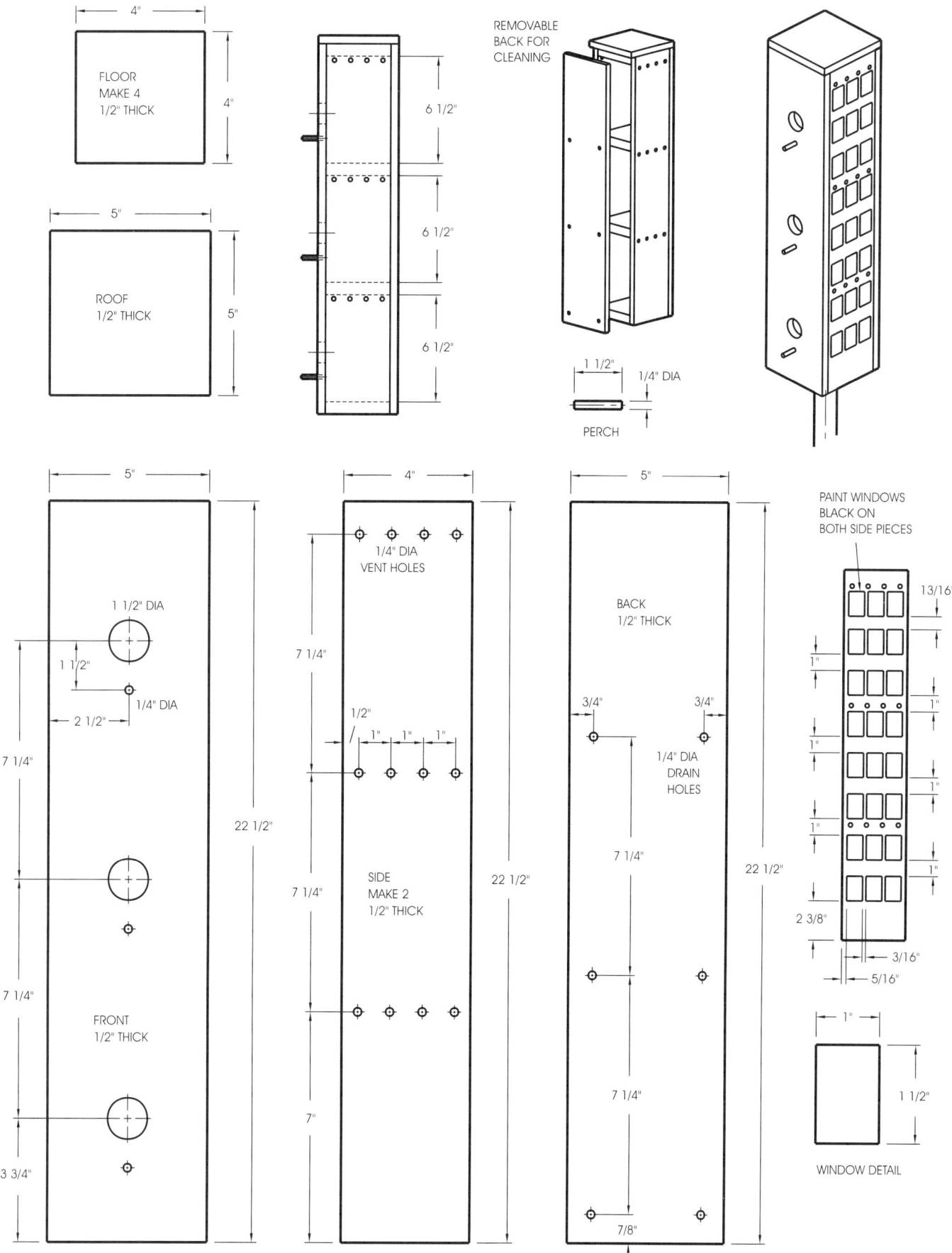

OLD WESTERN BUILDING BIRDHOUSE

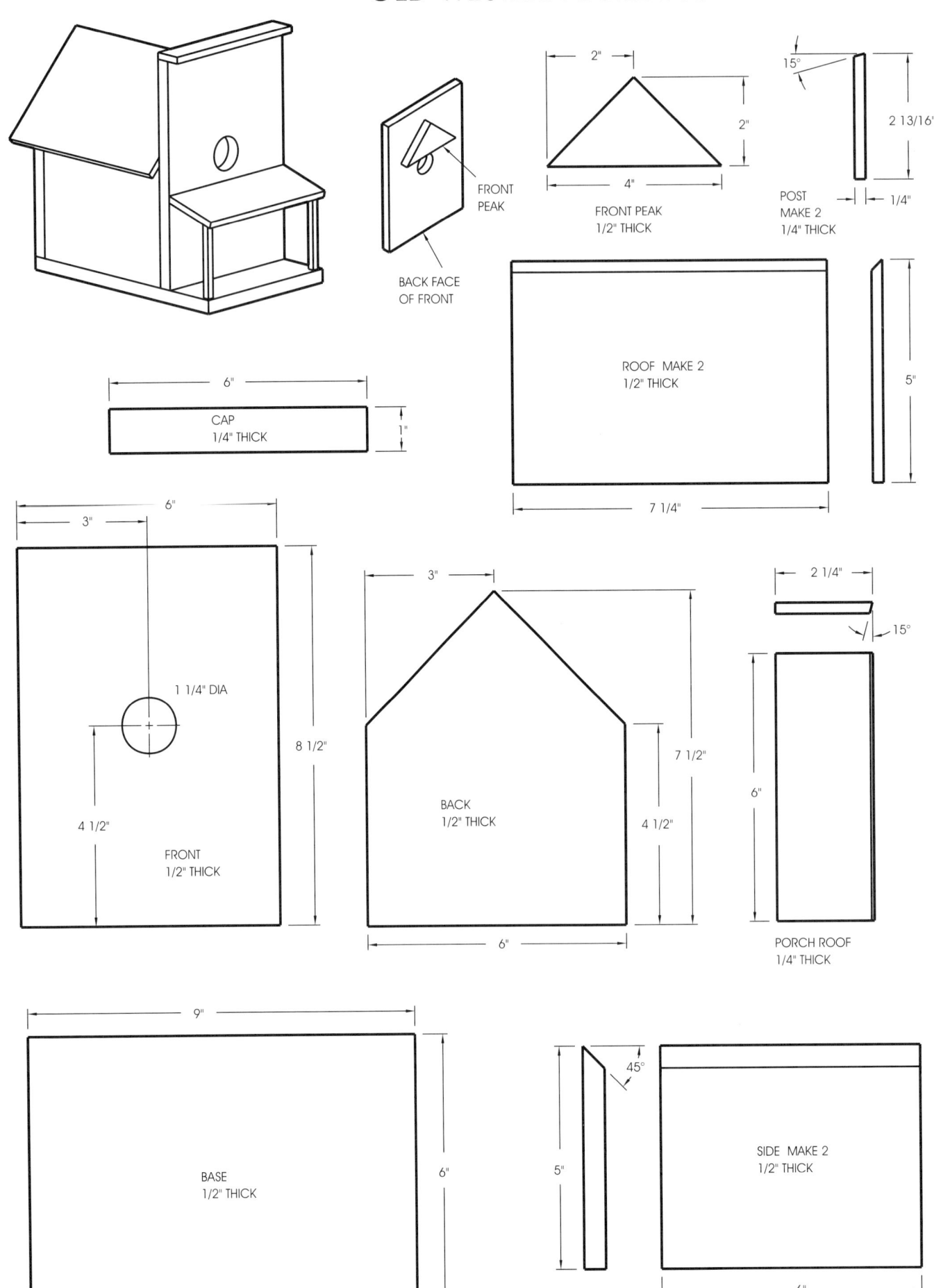

RAILROAD CRUMMY BIRDHOUSE

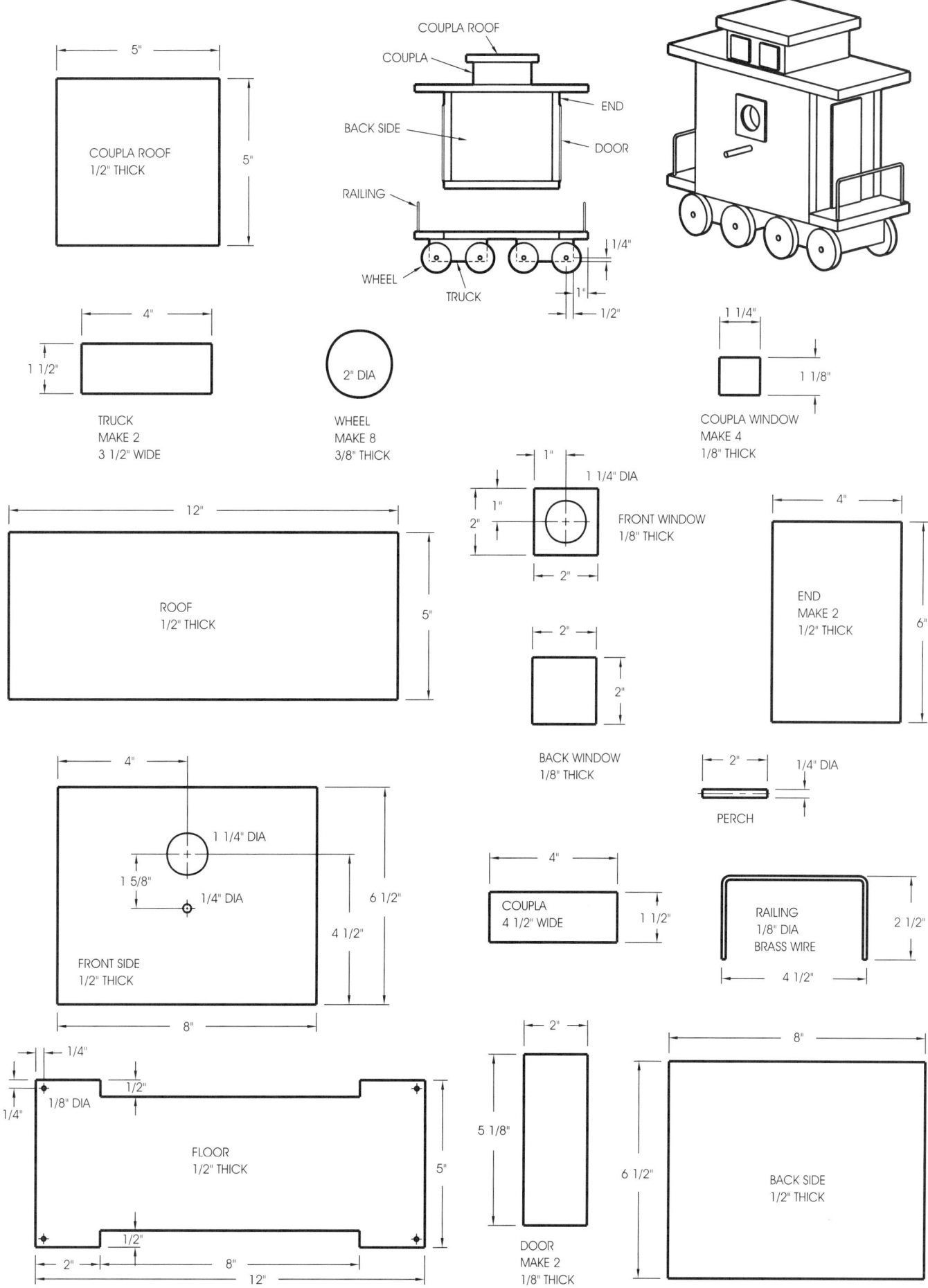

OLD HOUSE BIRDHOUSE

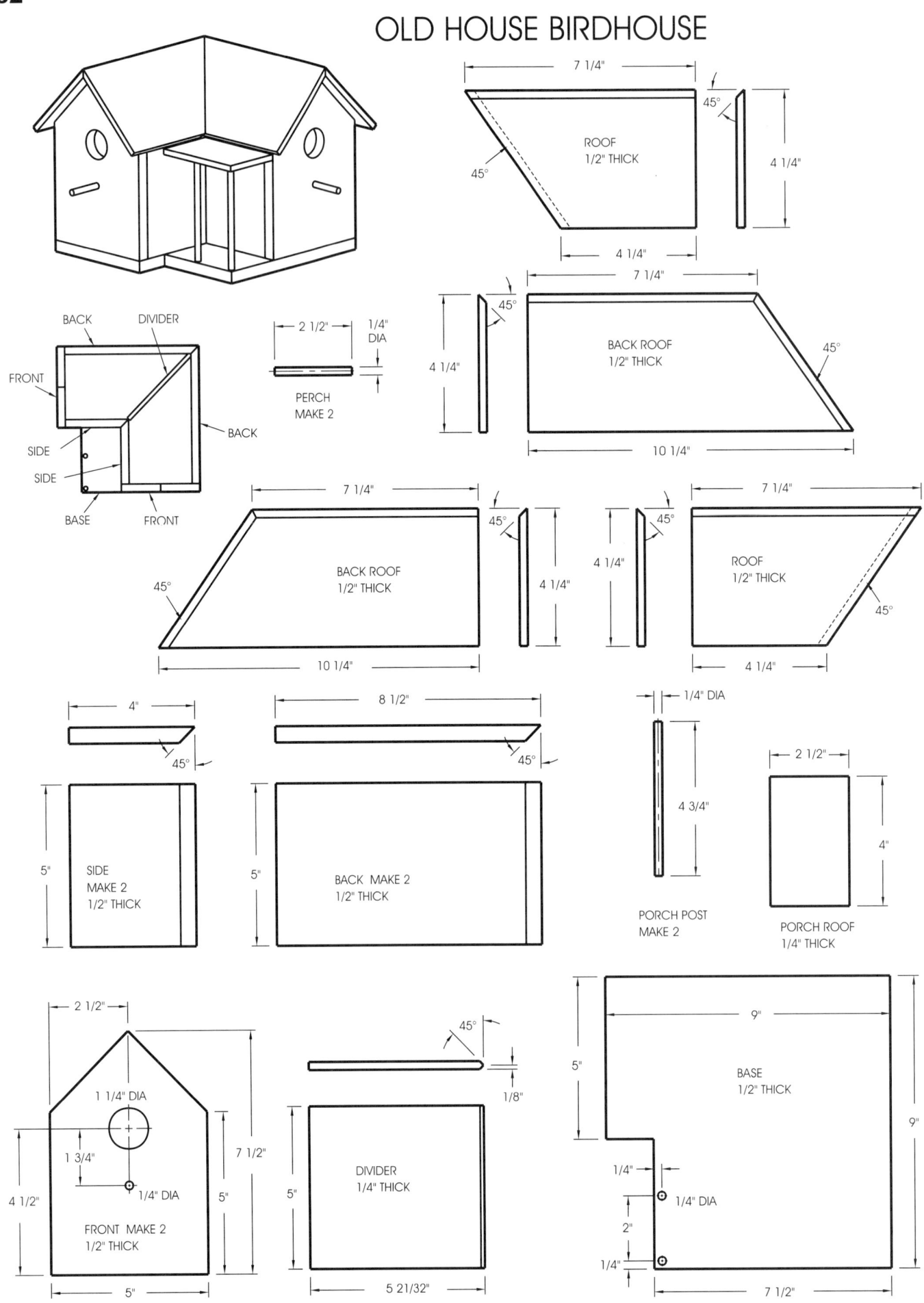

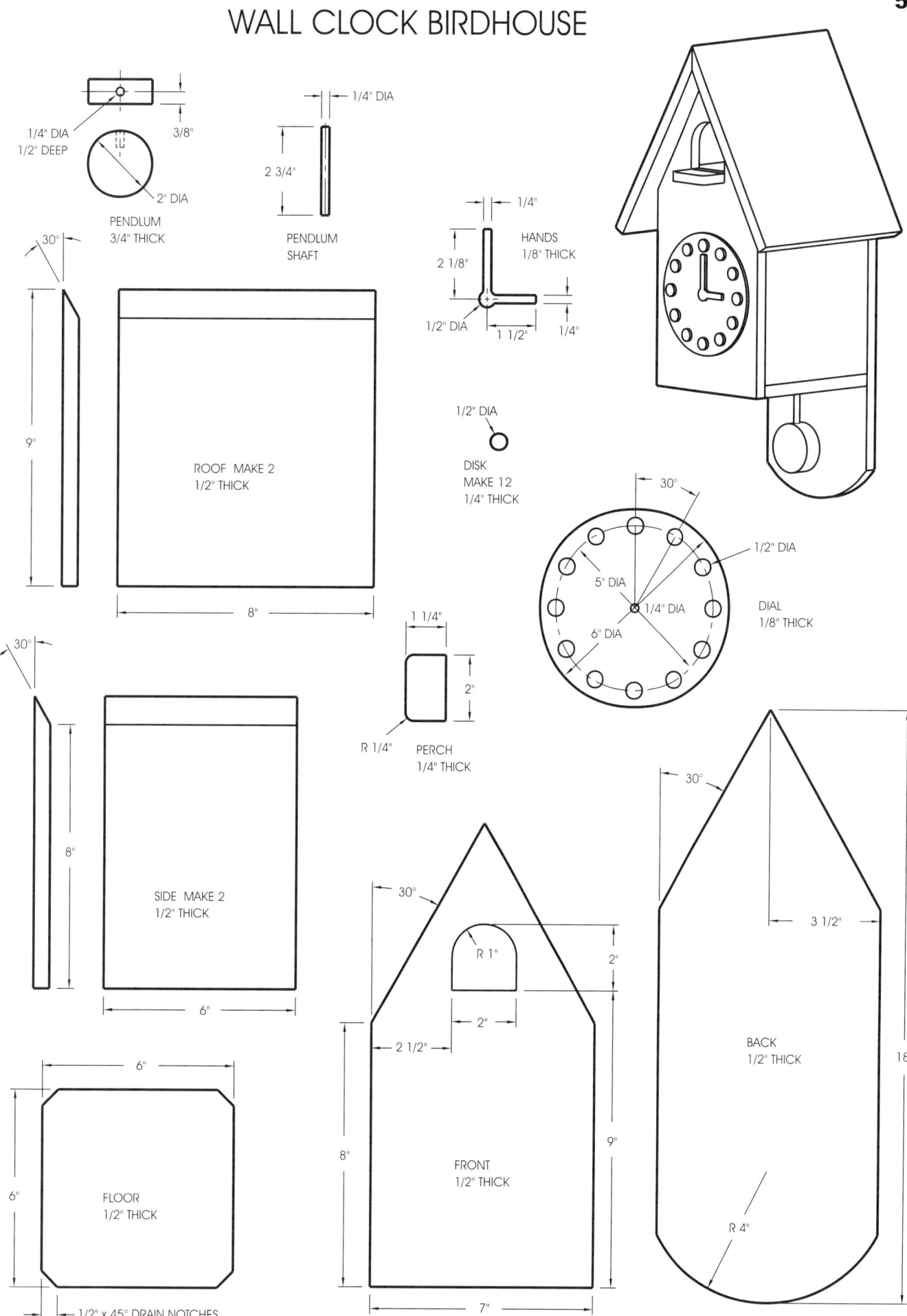

SHINGLE ROOF BIRDHOUSE

REMOVABLE FLOOR FOR CLEANING

ROOF CAP
MAKE 2
1/4" THICK
9"
1 3/4"
34°

ROOF
MAKE 6
1/4" THICK
9"
1 3/4"

FRONT
1/2" THICK
9 3/8"
1 1/4"
1 1/4"
1 1/4"
1/4"
5/8"
1 1/4" DIA
1 1/2"
1/4" DIA
5 3/4"
3 1/8"
6 5/32"
6 1/4"

SIDE
MAKE 2
1/2" THICK
34°
6 11/32"
6"

BACK
1/2" THICK
9 3/8"
1 1/4"
1 1/4"
1 1/4"
5/8"
1/4"
3 1/8"
6 1/8"
6 1/4"

PERCH
1 3/4"
1/4" DIA

FLOOR
1/2" THICK
5 1/4"
6"
1/2" x 45° DRAIN NOTCHES

PVC PIPE BIRD FEEDER

HANGING BIRDHOUSE FROM LOGS

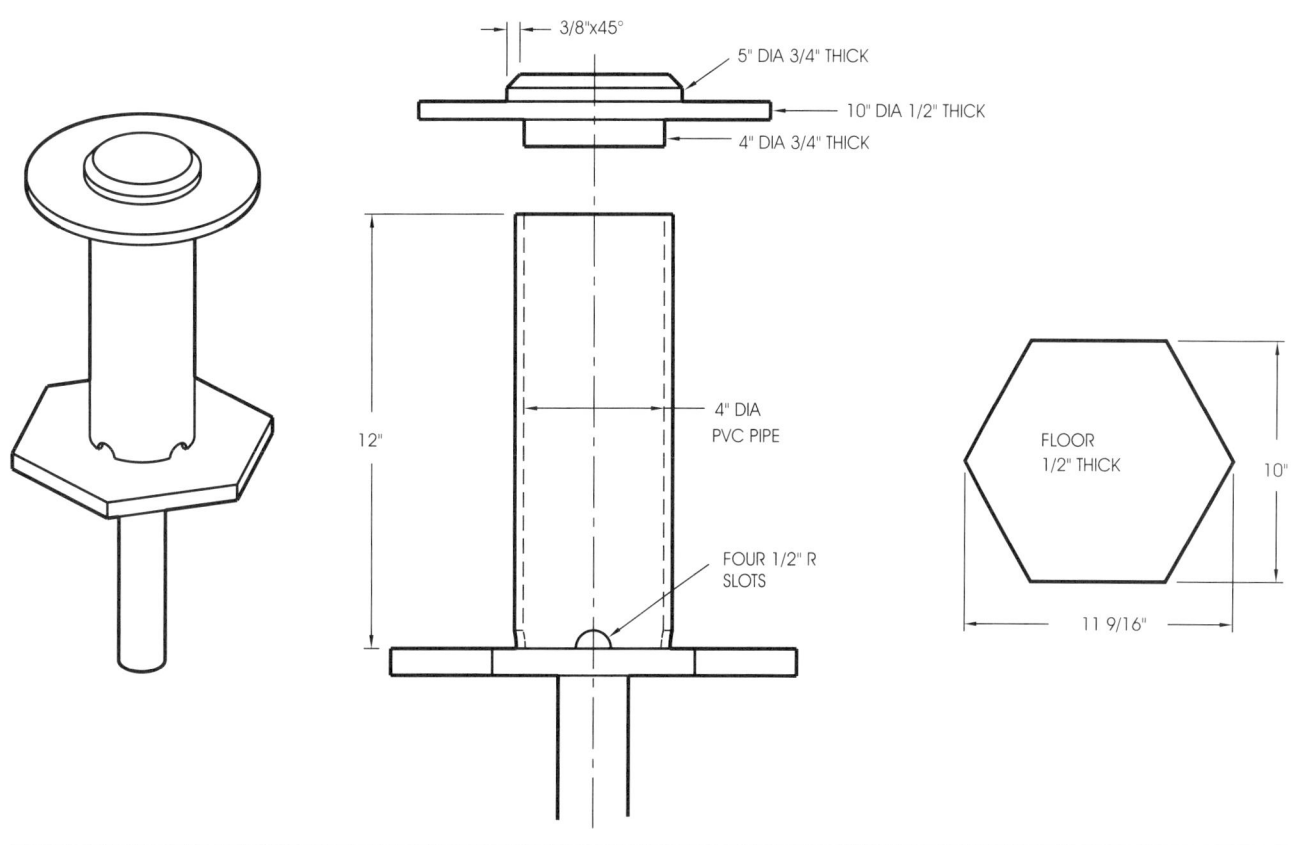

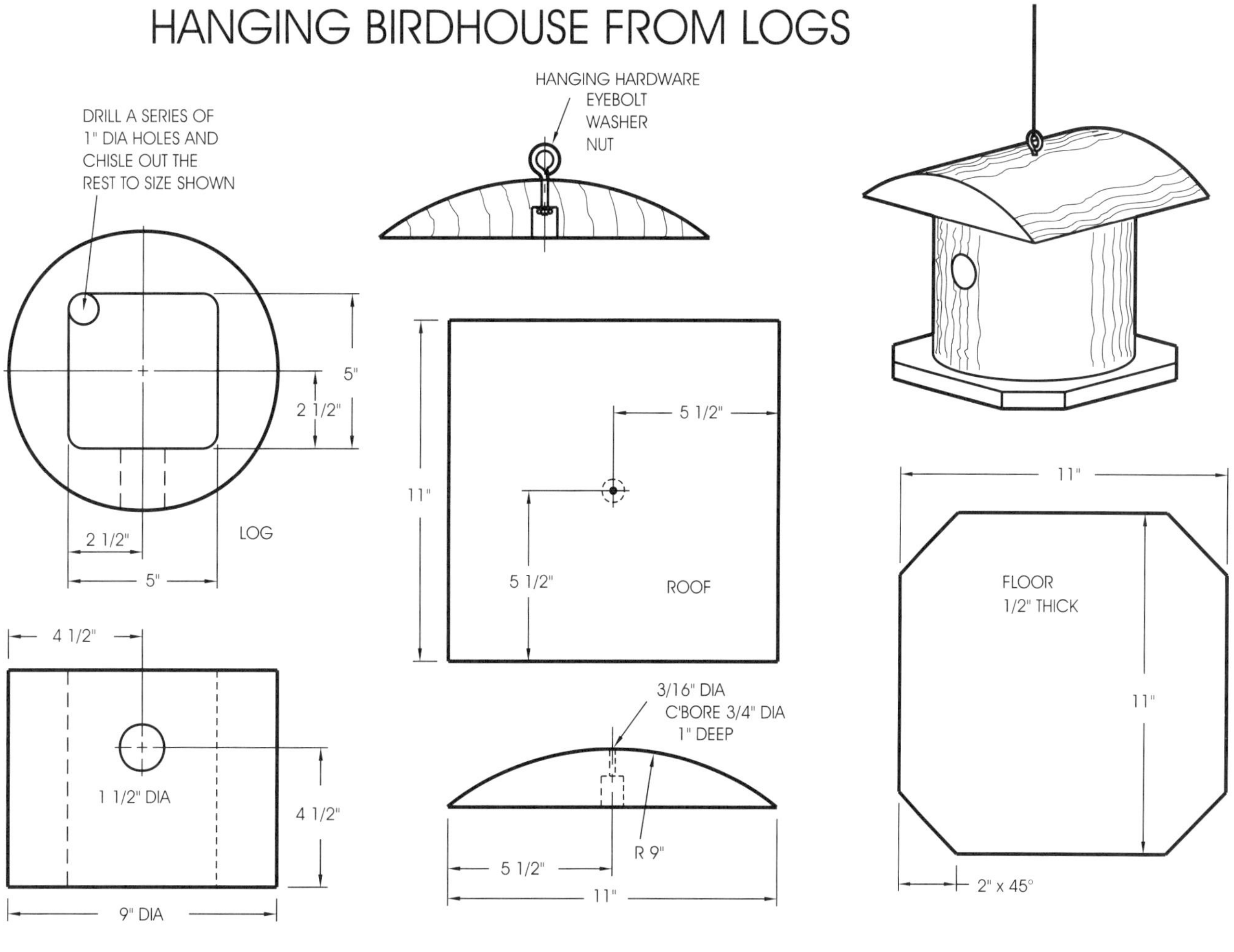

TRIANGLE BIRDHOUSE

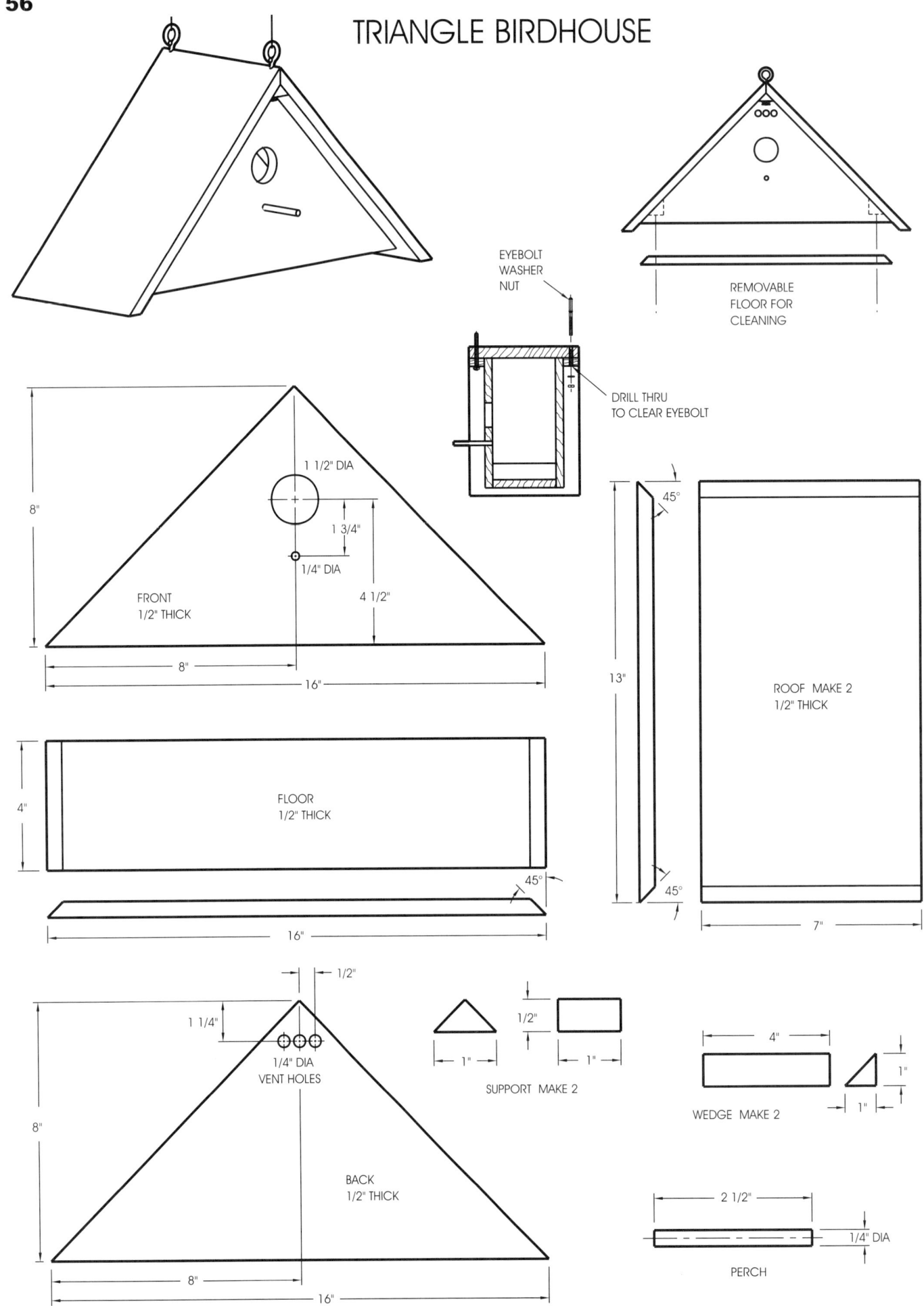

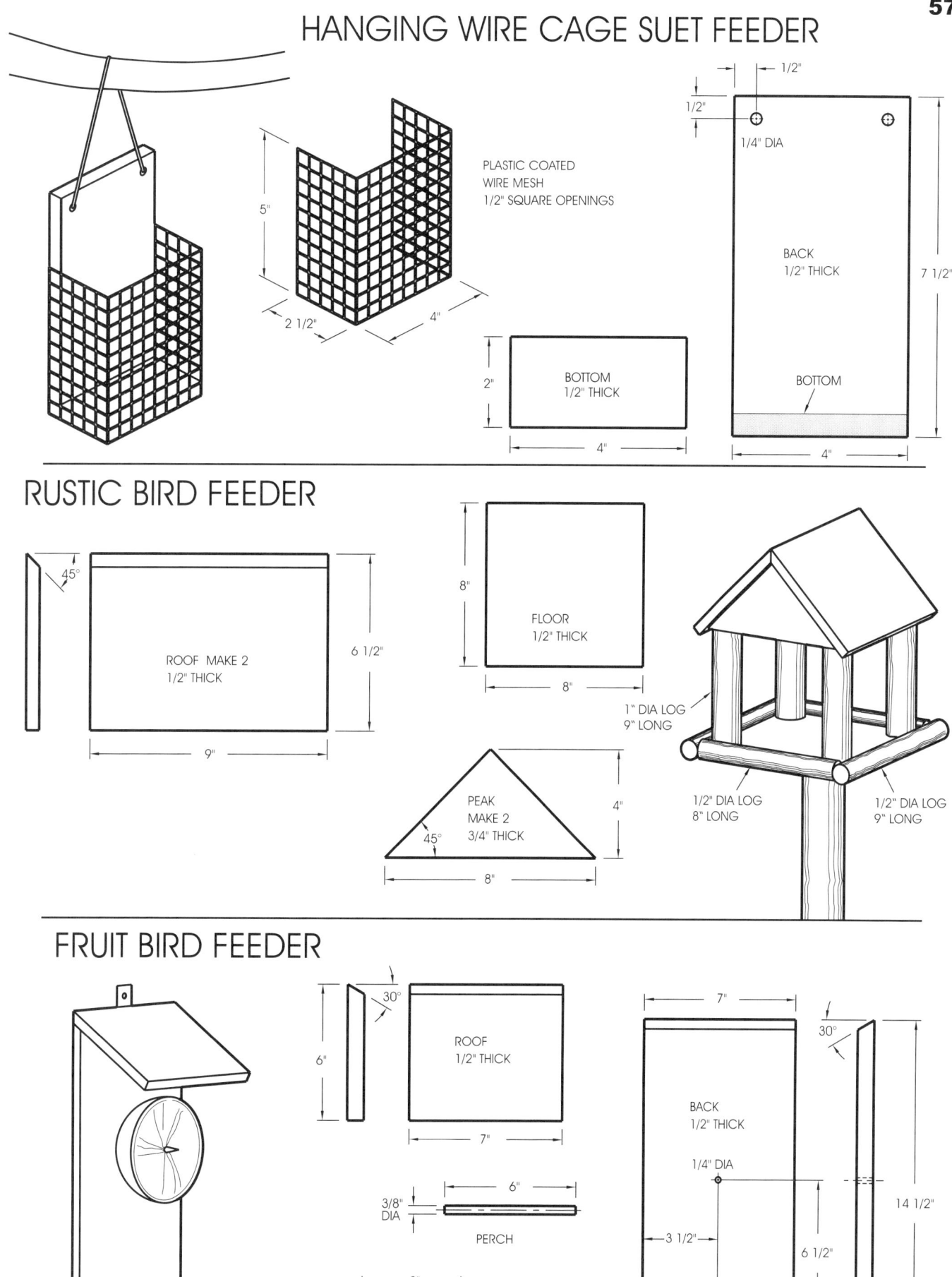

BIRD FEEDER OF LOGS

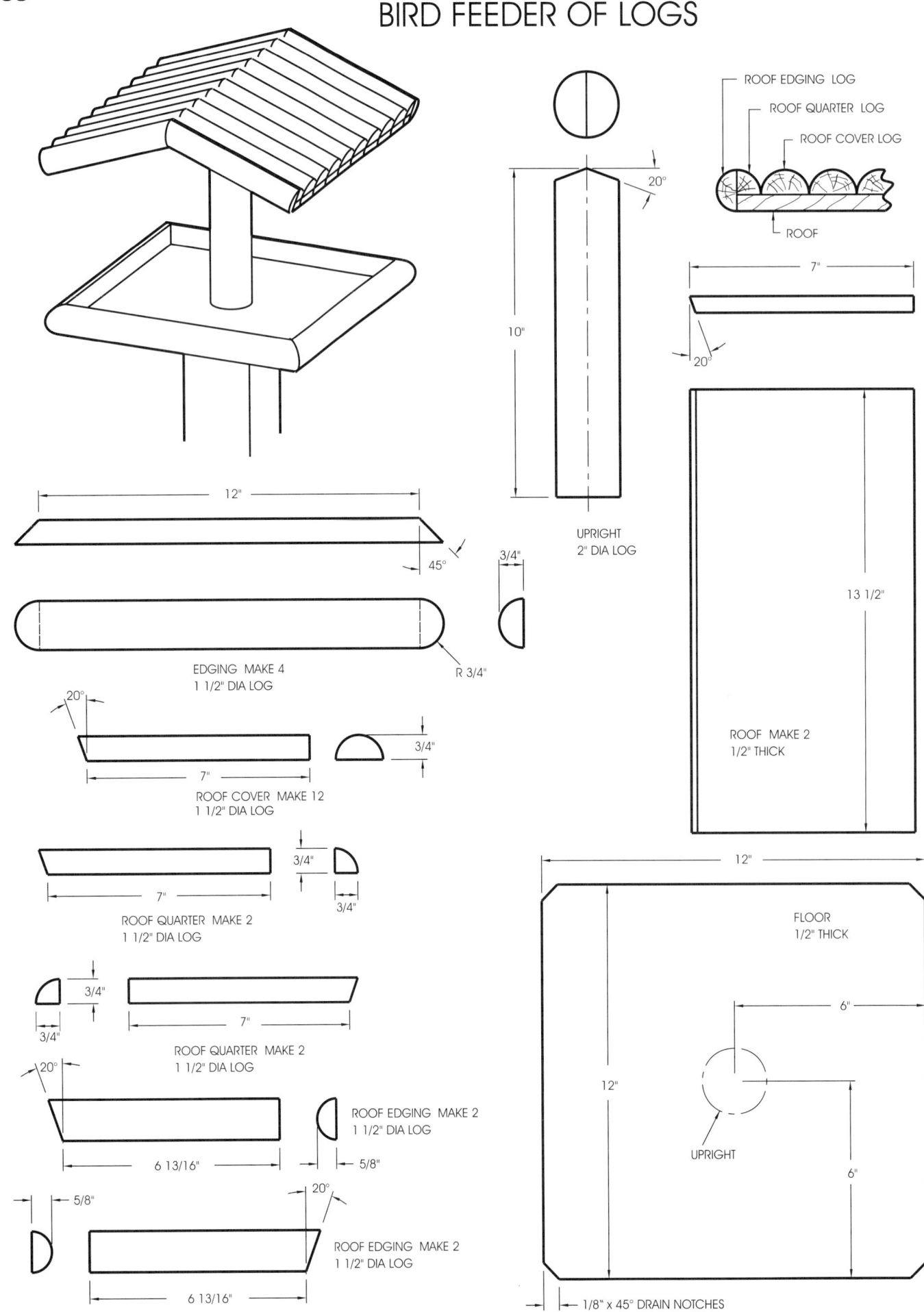

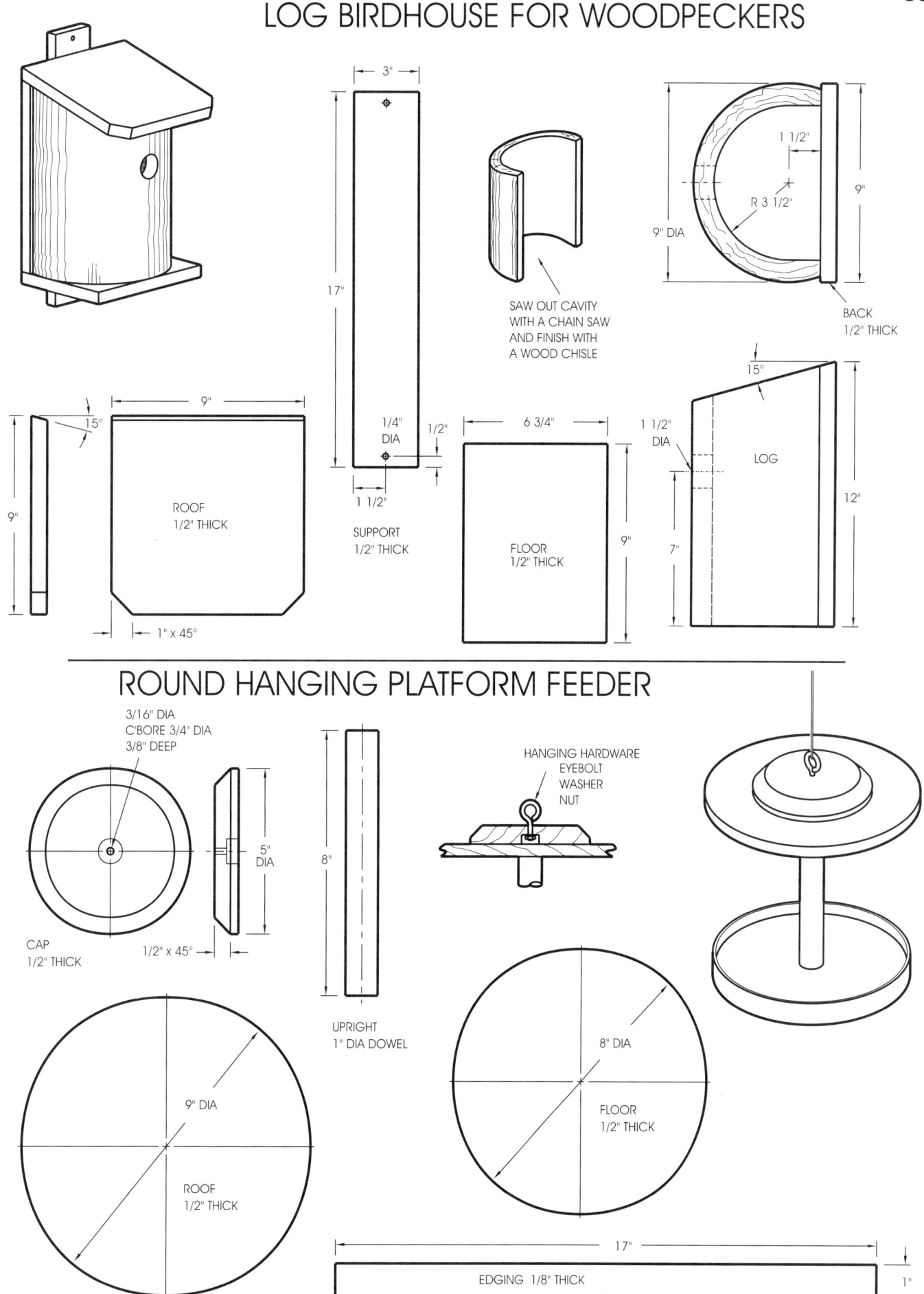

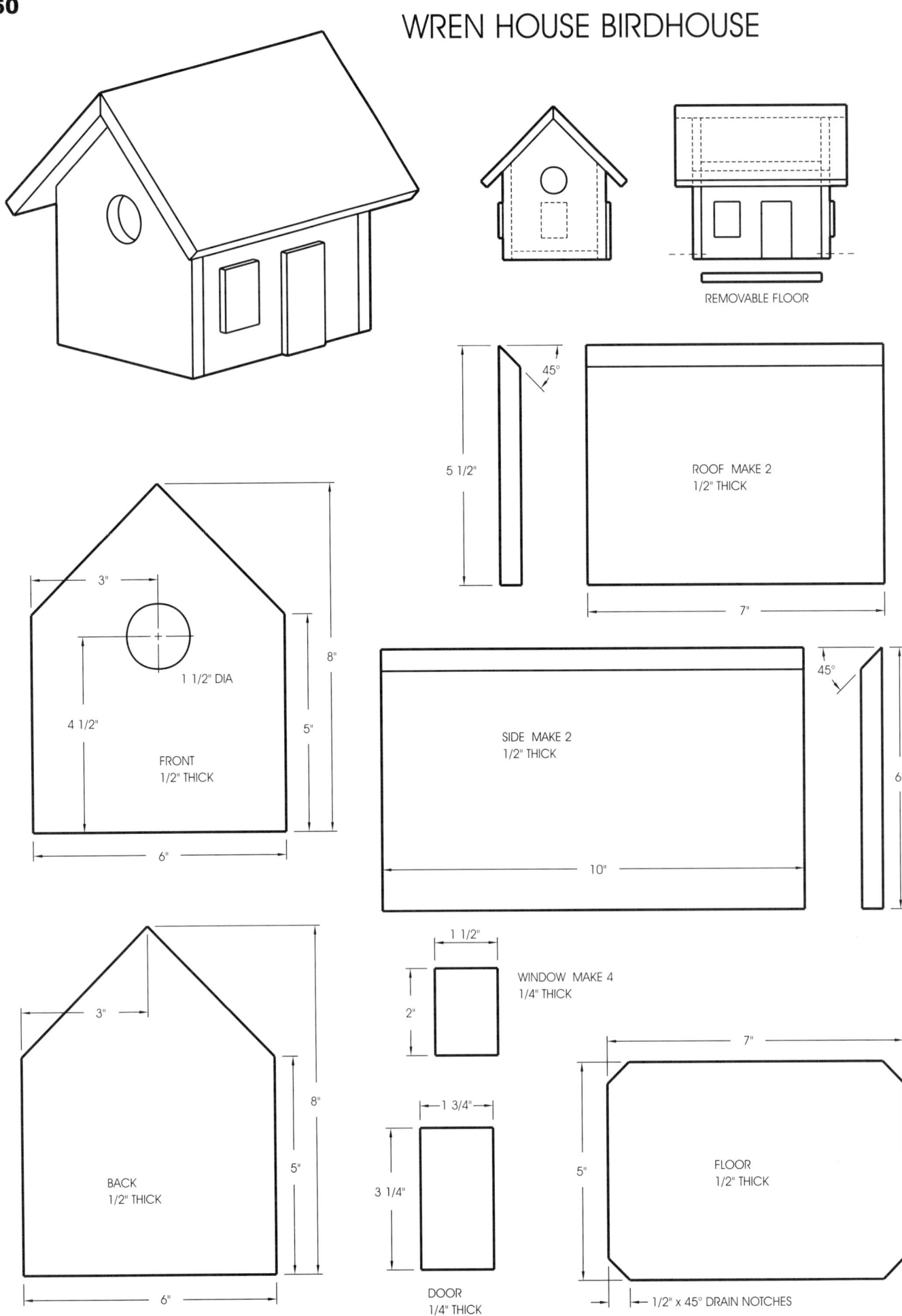

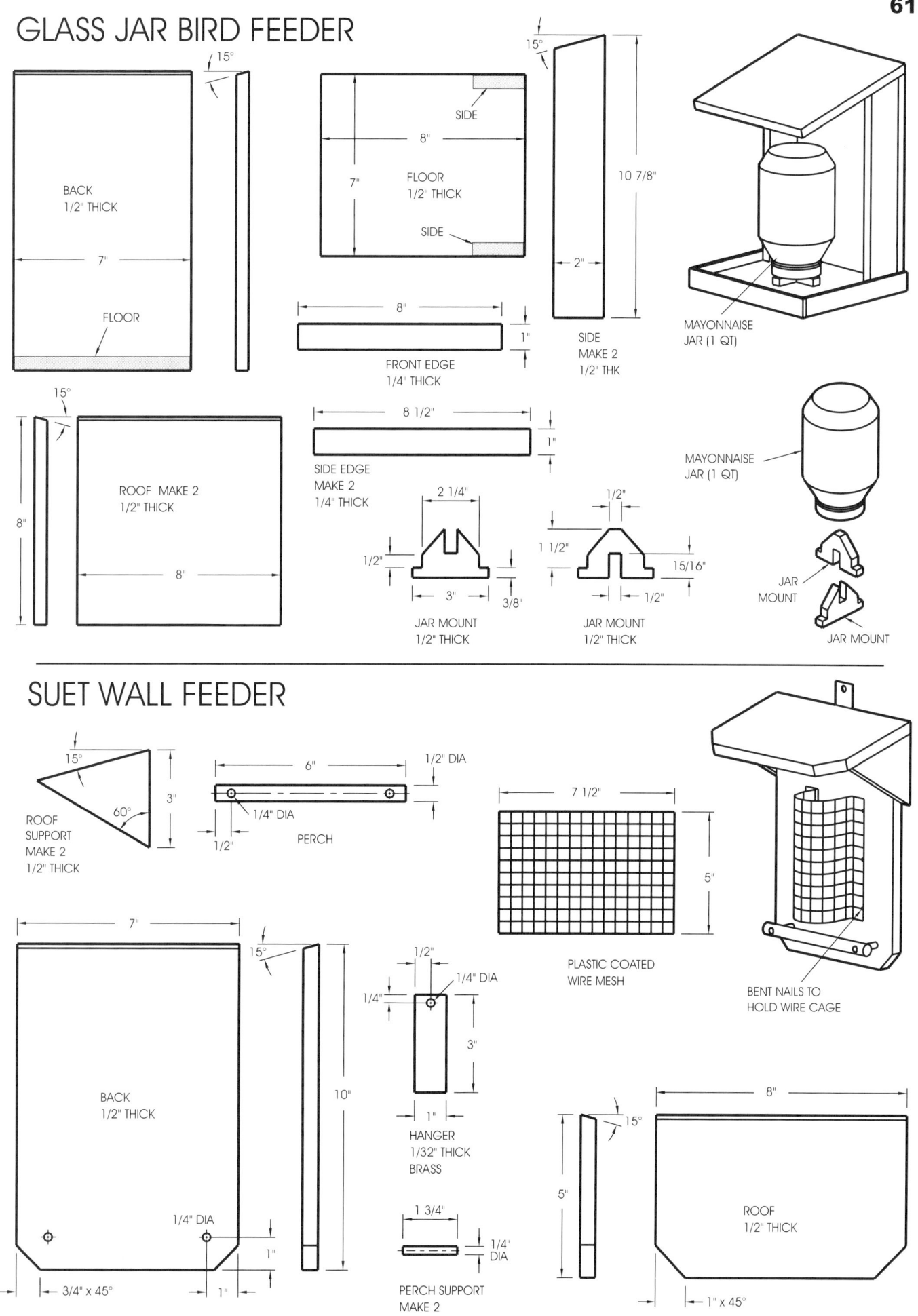

SUET LOG BIRD FEEDER

EYEBOLT
WASHER
NUT

BODY
TREE LIMB

1" DIA
3/4" DEEP

2"

4"

10"

3" DIA

4"

4"

3/16" DIA
C'BORE .75" DIA
3/8" DEEP

1/2" x 45°

ROOF
1/2" THICK

5" DIA

HANGING WATER BATH

WALL BIRD FEEDER

15°

6"

60°

5"

15°

10"

4"

8"

7"

3"

3"

S-HOOK 3 REQ'D
DRILL 3 HOLES IN DISH

14" DIA TERRA COTTA DISH

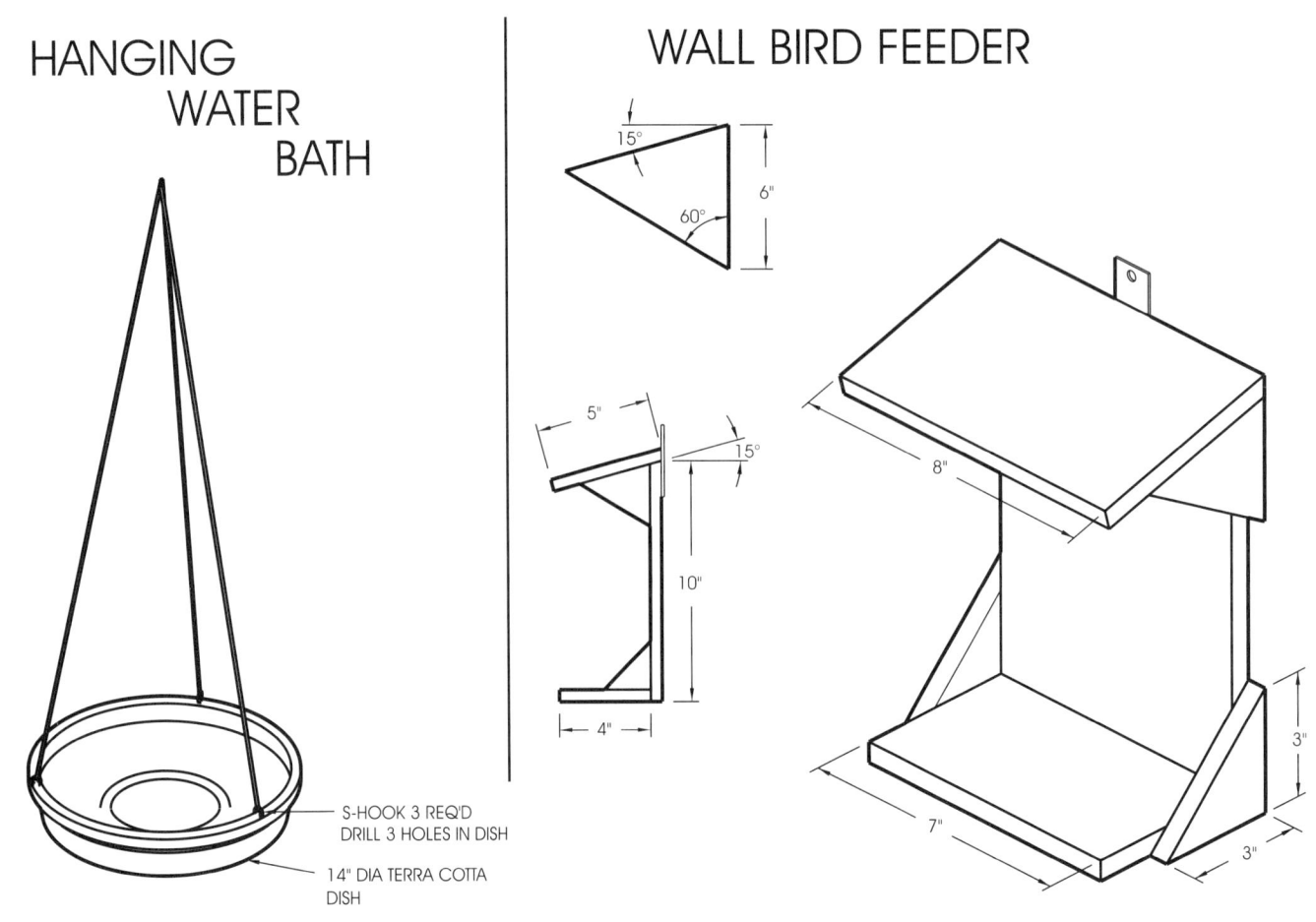

Birdhouse Size Requirements

Types	Entrance Diameter (inches)	Entrance above Floor (inches)	Interior Height of House (inches)	Floor of House (inches)	Height above Ground (feet)
Bluebird					
Eastern	1 1/2	6	8	5 x 5	5 to 10
Mountian	1 1/2	6	8	5 x 5	5 to 10
Western	1 1/2	6	8	5 x 5	5 to 10
Chickadee					
Black-capped	1 1/8	6 to 8	8 to 10	4 x 4	6 to 15
Carolina	1 1/8	6 to 8	8 to 10	4 x 4	6 to 15
Chestnut-backed	1 1/8	6 to 8	8 to 10	4 x 4	6 to 15
Gray-headed	1 1/8	6 to 8	8 to 10	4 x 4	6 to 15
Finch					
House	2	3 to 4	6	6 x 6	8 to 12
Flycatchers					
Great-crested	2	6 to 8	8 to 10	6 x 6	8 to 20
Western	2	6 to 8	8 to 10	6 x 6	8 to 20
Kestrel	3	9 to 12	12 to 15	8 x 8	10 to 30
Martin	2 1/2				
Purple	2	1	6	6 x 6	15 to 20
Western	2	1	6	6 x 6	15 to 20
Nuthatch					
Red-breasted	1 1/4	6 to 8	6 to 8	4 X 4	5 to 20
White-breasted	1 1/4	6 to 8	6 to 8	4 X 4	5 to 20
Owl					
Barn	6	4	15 to 18	10 x 18	12 to 18
Barred	8		16	13 x 15	10 to 30
Screech	3	9 to 12	12 to 15	8 x 8	10 to 30
Sparrows					
House	1 1/2	6	15	10 x 10	10 to 20
Song	all sides open		8 to 10	6 x 6	1 to 3
Swallows					
Tree	1 1/2	1 to 5	6	5 x 5	10 to 15
Titmouse					
Plain	1 1/4	6 to 8	8 to 10	4 x 4	6 to 15
Tufted	1 1/4	6 to 8	8 to 10	4 x 4	6 to 15
Warbler	1 1/2	5	8	4 x 4	4 to 7
Woodpecker					
Downy	1 1/4	6 to 8	8 to 10	4 x 4	6 to 20
Golden front	2	9 to 12	12 to 15	6 x 6	12 to 20
Hairy	1 1/2	9 to 12	12 to 15	6 x 6	12 to 20
Red-bellied	2 1/2	10 to 12	12 to 15	6 x 6	12 to 20
Redheaded	2	9 to 12	12 to 15	6 x 6	12 to 20
Wren					
Bewick's	1	1 to 6	6 to 8	4 x 4	6 to 10
Carolina	1 1/8	1 to 6	6 to 8	4 x 4	6 to 10
House	1	1 to 6	6 to 8	4 x 4	6 to 10
Winter	1 x 2 1/2	4 to 6	6 to 8	4 x 4	5 to 10

Index

A
Adobe Birdhouse, 41
A-Frame Birdhouse, 23
Authors' Notes, 4

B
Barn Birdhouse for Wrens, 18
Bird Feeder of Logs, 58
Bird Feeding Table, 43
Birdhouse Size Requirements, 63
Birdhouse for Tree Swallows, 33
Bluebird Birdhouse, 8
Birdhouse
   16-Apartment Martin Birdhouse, 28
   18-Apartment Martin Birdhouse, 44
   8-Sided Martin Birdhouse, 38
   Adobe Birdhouse, 41
   A-Frame Birdhouse, 23
   Barn Birdhouse for Wrens, 18
   Birdhouse Dimension Specifications, 63
   Birdhouse for Tree Swallows, 33
   Bluebird Birdhouse, 8
   Church Birdhouse, 26, 37
   Diamond Birdhouse for Wrens, 9
   Dove Cove, 25
   Eight-Apartment Martin Birdhouse, 20
   Farm House Birdhouse, 29
   Flower Pot Birdhouse, 16
   Hanging Birdhouse from Logs, 55
   Log Birdhouse for Woodpeckers, 59
   Log Cabin Birdhouse, 13
   Log House Birdhouse, 36
   Log Shed Birdhouse, 32
   Mailbox Birdhouse, 27
   Modern High-Rise Building Birdhouse, 49
   Nesting Shelf, 43
   Old House Birdhouse, 52
   Old Western Building Birdhouse, 50
   PVC Pipe Birdhouse, 16
   Railroad Crummy Birdhouse, 51
   Robin Nesting Shelf, 35
   School House Birdhouse, 24
   Shingle Roof Birdhouse, 54
   Slab Log Cabin Birdhouse, 48
   Three-Tier Birdhouse for Wrens, 11
   Tree Swallow Birdhouse, 34
   Triangle Birdhouse, 56
   Triangle Dove Cove, 40
   Typical Birdhouse, 6
   Two Dwelling Birdhouse, 42
   Wall Clock Birdhouse, 53
   Wall Mounted Nesting Shelf for Robins, 12
   Wren House Birdhouse, 60
Bird Feeder
   Bird Feeder of Logs, 58
   Bird Feeding Table, 43
   Four Post Bird Feeder, 46
   Fruit Bird Feeder, 57
   Glass Jar Bird Feeder, 61
   Hanging Bird Feeder, 14, 22
   Hanging Wire Cage Suet Feeder, 57
   Hopper Bird Feeder, 31
   Post Bird Feeder, 15, 30
   Post Mounted Hopper Bird Feeder, 17
   PVC Pipe Feeder, 55
   Round Hanging Platform Feeder, 59
   Rustic Bird Feeder, 57
   Small Hanging Bird Feeder, 5
   Suet Wall Feeder, 61
   Suet Log Bird Feeder, 62
   Three Station Bird Feeder, 19
   Three-Tier Bird Feeder, 47
   Wall Bird Feeder, 62
   Wall Mounted Bird Feeder, 10
   Window Bird Feeder, 16
Bird Bath
   Hanging Water Bath, 62

C
Church Birdhouse, 26, 37

D
Diamond Birdhouse for Wrens, 9
Dove Cove, 25

E
8-Sided Martin Birdhouse, 38
18-Apartment Martin Birdhouse, 44
Eight-Apartment Martin Birdhouse, 20

F
Farm House Birdhouse, 29
Flower-Pot Birdhouse, 16
Four Post Bird Feeder, 46
Fruit Bird Feeder, 57

G
Glass Jar Bird Feeder, 61

H
Hanging Birdhouse from Logs, 55
Hanging Bird Feeder, 14, 22
Hanging Water Bath, 62
Hanging Wire Cage Suet Feeder, 57
Hopper Bird Feeder, 31

L
Log Birdhouse for Woodpeckers, 59
Log Cabin Birdhouse, 13
Log House Birdhouse, 36
Log Shed Birdhouse, 32

M
Mailbox Birdhouse, 27
Modern High-Rise Building Birdhouse, 49

N
Nesting Shelf, 43

O
Old House Birdhouse, 52
Old Western Building Birdhouse, 50

P
Post Bird Feeder, 15, 30
Post Mounted Hopper Bird Feeder, 17
PVC Pipe Birdhouse, 16
PVC Pipe Bird Feeder, 55

R
Railroad Crummy Birdhouse, 51
Robin Nesting Shelf, 35
Round Hanging Platform Feeder, 59
Rustic Bird Bird Feeder, 57

S
16-Apartment Martin Birdhouse, 28
School House Birdhouse, 24
Shingle Roof Birdhouse, 54
Slab Log Cabin Birdhouse, 48
Small Hanging Bird Feeder, 5
Suet Wall Feeder, 61
Suet Log Bird Feeder, 62

T
Three Station Bird Feeder, 19
Three-Tier Birdhouse for Wrens, 11
Three-Tier Bird Feeder, 47
Tree Swallow Birdhouse, 34
Triangle Birdhouse, 56
Triangle Dove Cove, 40
Typical Birdhouse, 6
Two Dwelling Birdhouse, 42

W
Wall Bird Feeder, 62
Wall Clock Birdhouse, 53
Wall Mounted Bird Feeder, 10
Wall Mounted Bluebird Birdhouse, 7
Wall Mounted Nesting Shelf for Robins, 12
Window Bird Feeder, 16
Wren House Birdhouse, 60